If Your Adolescent Has Depression

THE ANNENBERG
PUBLIC POLICY CENTER
OF THE UNIVERSITY OF PENNSYLVANIA

Daniel Romer, PhD, Director of Research

The Annenberg Foundation Trust at
SUNNYLANDS

The Adolescent Mental Health Initiative of the Annenberg
Public Policy Center and the Sunnylands Trust

Patrick E. Jamieson, PhD, series editor

Other books in the series

If Your Adolescent Has Schizophrenia
Raquel E. Gur, MD, and Ann Braden Johnson, PhD

If Your Adolescent Has an Anxiety Disorder
Edna B. Foa, PhD, and Linda Wasmer Andrews

If Your Adolescent Has ADHD
Tomas J. Power, PhD, and Linda Wasmer Andrews

If Your Adolescent Has an Eating Disorder
B. Timothy Walsh, MD, and Deborah R. Glasofer, PhD

If Your Adolescent Has Bipolar Disorder
Dwight L. Evans, MD, Tami D. Benton, MD,
and Katherine Ellison

If Your Adolescent Has Depression

An Essential Resource for Parents

Dwight L. Evans, MD, Moira A. Rynn, MD, and
Katherine Ellison

THE ANNENBERG
PUBLIC POLICY CENTER
OF THE UNIVERSITY OF PENNSYLVANIA

The Adolescent Mental Health Initiative of the Annenberg
Public Policy Center and the Sunnylands Trust

The Annenberg Foundation Trust at
SUNNYLANDS

OXFORD
UNIVERSITY PRESS

OXFORD
UNIVERSITY PRESS

Oxford University Press is a department of the University of Oxford. It furthers
the University's objective of excellence in research, scholarship, and education
by publishing worldwide. Oxford is a registered trade mark of Oxford University
Press in the UK and certain other countries.

Published in the United States of America by Oxford University Press
198 Madison Avenue, New York, NY 10016, United States of America.

© Oxford University Press 2023

First edition published as *If Your Adolescent Has Depression or Bipolar Disorder: An Essential
Resource for Parents*, by Dwight L. Evans, MD, and Linda Wasmer Andrews (Oxford
University Press, 2005)

Library of Congress Cataloging-in-Publication Data
Names: Evans, Dwight L., author. | Rynn, Moira A., author. |
Ellison, Katherine, 1957– author.
Title: If your adolescent has depression : an essential resource for parents /
Dwight L. Evans, Moira A. Rynn, and Katherine Ellison.
Description: New York, NY : Oxford University Press, [2023] |
Series: The adolescent mental health initiative of the Annenberg Public Policy Center and
the Sunnylands Trust | Includes bibliographical references.
Identifiers: LCCN 2022049854 (print) | LCCN 2022049855 (ebook) |
ISBN 9780197636060 (hardback) | ISBN 9780197636077 (paperback) |
ISBN 9780197636091 (epub) | ISBN 9780197636107 (ebook)
Subjects: LCSH: Depression in adolescence—Popular works. | Depression in
adolescence—Treatment—Popular works. | Parent and teenager—Popular works.
Classification: LCC RJ506.D4 E928 2023 (print) | LCC RJ506.D4 (ebook) |
DDC 616.85/2700835—dc23/eng/20230210
LC record available at https://lccn.loc.gov/2022049854
LC ebook record available at https://lccn.loc.gov/2022049855

DOI: 10.1093/med-psych/9780197636060.001.0001

Paperback printed by Sheridan Books, Inc., United States of America
Hardback printed by Bridgeport National Bindery, Inc., United States of America

Contents

Six
Sex, Drugs, and Social Media   130

Seven
Surviving School   152

Eight
Life After High School   181

Nine
Coping With Crises   193

Conclusion: Hope on the Horizon   217

Introduction

More Than Merely Moody

Raising an adolescent is rarely a breeze. Your child's brain and body are changing profoundly and quickly. Fluctuating hormones spark emotional storms. It's all part of the bargain you didn't know you'd made when you first held that tiny infant in your arms.

Most parents manage to navigate the ups and downs, trusting they won't last forever. Yet sometimes dramatic changes in moods are wake-up calls to a more serious problem: namely, clinical depression, otherwise known as major depressive disorder.

Depression can be mild or severe. Many kids learn to manage it on their own. Yet millions of parents have been caught off guard by a non-negotiable signal that they need to step in. If you've picked up this book, you may recognize the shock these parents felt when they first saw that red flag:

> "Jenny was 13 when I brought her in for a regular check-up with her pediatrician," says her father, Miles. "The doctor called me in to show me all the scars on her arm, where she had been cutting herself with a razor."

Maybe your child has put you on notice more subtly. Perhaps your son recently quit his after-school baseball team and has been sleeping later than usual. Or your formerly sunny daughter has been pleading to stay home from school, complaining of mysterious aches and pains.

Young people have lots of good reason to be moody these days, apart from their changing biochemistry. Climate change, income inequality, increasing competition for jobs, and a lot of disturbing, nonstop content on social media all likely help explain some of the recent uptick in depression and anxiety in adolescents. In a mostly positive development, young people today are also more willing to talk about problems that used to be too shameful to reveal. In this book, however, we'll focus on how genes, trauma, and stress can help turn common worries into clinical-grade suffering that needs your prompt attention. This is the case when sorrow, hopelessness, or apathy lasts more than a couple of weeks, interfering with life at home, school, or work.

Doctors who treat adolescents once believed they were immune to clinical depression. Only in recent decades has there been wide acceptance that children may suffer this illness. Indeed, we now know that depression often first appears during the adolescent and young adult years, and sometimes even before puberty. In adolescents, just as in adults, it can be a serious, long-lasting, and recurring problem.

The Company You Keep

As someone who loves someone who is clinically depressed, you may already know you're not alone. Depression was already one of the most common mental illnesses worldwide out of distress. Helping to lift a child's mood can take time, and you are dealing with a medical system that by many accounts is broken.

Parents often feel frustrated as they absorb just how different psychiatry is from orthopedics or cardiovascular surgery. While mental illnesses often have physical symptoms, there is much more variation, subjectivity—and, often, controversy— surrounding approaches to address them. Mental health treatments are often more complex and multilayered than setting a bone or repairing a leaky valve, involving learned habits, environments, and thinking styles. To give your child the best chance of success, you'll need to educate yourself. A basic understanding of diagnoses and treatments will help you choose a specialist, know the right questions to ask, and understand the advice you get.

Without wishing to scare you, we do want to emphasize the high stakes.

Depressed adolescents are considerably more likely than others to intentionally injure themselves, including attempting suicide, a risk that has been tragically increasing. In recent years, suicide has become the second leading cause of death for this age group. The US suicide rate for those aged 10 to 24 rose by more than 57% from 2007 to 2018—up to nearly 11 youth per 100,000. And that was before COVID-19.

Knowledge Is Power

The news may be grim, but remember: Depression is a treatable illness. In the following pages, we'll empower you with lots of practical information and suggestions. Among other things, we'll tell you how to recognize depression, what treatments are available, how you can help prevent relapses and reduce the symptoms, how you can find a therapist, how you can help your child at home and at school, and what to do in an emergency. We'll give you the most up-to-date guidance on how to be a smart health care consumer, including information on the safety and side-effects of common medications, how to figure out the right kind of medical insurance, and how to find financial support if you can't afford insurance. We'll describe the risks of consuming alcohol, recreational drugs, and social media, and suggest how to reduce stress at home. We'll also explain how to understand and establish an individualized education program at school, and how best to prepare your child for life after high school. Finally, we'll offer some language to speak openly about mental illness and health with your child, as well as with anyone else in your world who may need to know what's going on.

Throughout the book, you'll hear from credentialed experts and also from many ordinary parents throughout America— and a few of their children—who have walked this road before you and learned from their experiences. We found our brain trust through a variety of sources. Some parents were active on social media; others were personal friends and acquaintances; some were patients; still others were authors who have written about their children's struggles. Some were interviewed while amid heart breaking struggles. Others, with their children grown, were able to look back calmly on the choices that helped them endure. In several cases, we follow their stories all the way through the book. To protect their privacy in all but a few cases, we changed their names, but we used their quotes verbatim. The one question we asked all of them was: "What did you learn?"

Reasons for Hope

There are many reasons for worry, but we also have a lot of good news to share as you embark on this journey with your child. Many parents manage to find compassionate and effective help from professionals willing to go well beyond the call of duty. Some have even found insurance-plan managers keen to ensure they're getting all the help they need.

Another bright sign is the sharp decrease in recent years in misinformation and stigma surrounding mental illness.

For centuries, people with severe depression or other mental illnesses were thought to be possessed by evil spirits. Exorcism and bloodletting were once among cutting-edge treatments. Even in recent decades, mental health experts wrongly cast blame for mental illnesses and behavioral disorders like autism and attention-deficit/hyperactivity disorder (ADHD) on bad parenting—and most often on bad *mothering*. Many people suffering depression resisted talking openly about their struggles, out of a reasonable fear that they'd be blamed and ostracized.

In the last several years, there's been a sea change, however, with many national campaigns against stigma, including "Make It OK" and "Bring Change to Mind." A thriving genre of movies, including *Little Miss Sunshine*, *Girl Interrupted*, and *Inside Out*; podcasts, like "The Hilarious World of Depression"; and even musicals, including *Dear Evan Hansen* and *Next to Normal*, have contributed to this movement. A brave procession of famous people has meanwhile shared their stories of mental illness in memoir after memoir, and in interviews with traditional and social media. They include writers, musicians, actors, politicians, athletes, and royal family members who've opened up about what it's like to suffer—and cope with—depression.

> "I slept all the time . . . because sleeping was basically better than offing myself," Olympic gymnast Simone Biles said of the depression she suffered after being sexually abused by former USA Gymnastics team doctor Larry Nassar.

> "I felt like I was behind a veil," TV producer Oprah Winfrey said of a depression that lasted six weeks. "I felt like what many people had described over the years on my show, and I could never imagine it. What's depression? Why don't you just pick yourself up?"

> "I'm on a variety of medications that keep me on an even keel; otherwise I can swing rather dramatically and . . . just the wheels can come off a little bit," said rock star Bruce Springsteen.

None of this implies that stigma has vanished. But it's never been less of an obstacle, which makes your job much easier.

And here is the best news of all: Adolescents' brains are changing and growing all the time—most often, believe it or not, for the better. Sometimes all a parent needs to do is keep showing love and maintain communication until the crises pass. Of course, it's still enormously demanding to be constantly worried about your child's safety, while helping someone who may be at least temporarily incapable of showing much love in return. But as we hope to show you, there are lots of ways to lighten the load.

Welcome to the Journey

Some parents of children with depression describe their challenge AS a spiritual journey—a helpful way to reframe all that stress and unpaid labor. As you embark, we hope to be your straight-talking companion and practical guide. We understand how much you may need a nonjudgmental friend.

> "This is an isolating experience because you do not feel you can share this with people, and it is isolating because when you do share it with others they do not understand," says Maria, who sought help for her 14-year-old daughter, Lourdes, after she withdrew and lost interest in school.

> "It's hard to find other parents of kids with a mental illness, because who the hell wants to advertise it?" writes "MichiganMom," in an online essay. "Oh, your kid is on the debate team? That's great. My son was nearly institutionalized for being suicidal and I had to take away anything sharp and his belts from his room. Want to meet for coffee and chat about it? No, not likely."

Like many other parents, Maria and MichiganMom found solace through friendships with other mothers whose children were similarly struggling. We urge you to track down these online and in-real-life (IRL) friendships as well.

> "It was such a comfort to know that I was not alone, that these moms get it, that I had a place to pour it all out to parents who had been there and survived," writes MichiganMom. "These parents are my lifeline and my heroes."

There is comfort in numbers, even as the numbers are increasing. But the bottom line is that *you* can make a critical difference at this critical time in your child's life. And while from time to time you may feel frustrated, confused, or even overwhelmed, take heart. Our society is finally waking up to this crisis, and the prognosis for our youth is increasingly hopeful.

The Authors

This book has three coauthors.

Coauthor Dwight L. Evans, MD, sadly passed away as this book was going to press. He was the Joseph and Madonna DiGiacomo Professor of Psychiatry and Professor of Psychiatry, Medicine, and Neuroscience at the Perelman School of Medicine at the University of Pennsylvania. He was Chair of the Depression and Bipolar Commission of the Annenberg Adolescent Mental Health Initiative and past President of the American Foundation for Suicide Prevention and the American College of Psychiatrists.

Coauthor Moira A. Rynn, MD, an expert in the treatment of mood and anxiety disorders across the lifespan, is Chair of the Department of Psychiatry and Behavioral Sciences at Duke University School of Medicine. Dr. Rynn has served as a principal investigator or co-principal investigator on numerous controlled adult and pediatric clinical trials involving medication and psychosocial treatments and has led medication clinical trials in pediatric mood and anxiety disorders.

Coauthor Katherine Ellison is a Pulitzer Prize–winning former foreign correspondent and author and coauthor of 10 nonfiction books, who has specialized in reporting on mental health issues for the past two decades. Her articles on mental health (and other topics) have appeared in leading publications, including the *New York Times*, the *Washington Post, Scientific American*, and *Knowable Magazine*.

We are grateful to veteran science writer Linda Wasmer Andrews for her contributions to the book's first edition in 2005, which was titled *If Your Adolescent Has Depression or Bipolar Disorder*. Katherine would additionally like to thank the psychiatrists Michelle Guchereau, Kiki Chang, Jean Milofsky, and James Ellison; the psychologists Stephen Hinshaw and Archana Basu; and the education expert Patricia Howey for their consultations on the current edition.

All of us are particularly indebted to the many parents of children with depression throughout the country who became our brain trust, contributing their hard-won wisdom. We deeply appreciate their generosity in speaking with us.

No pharmaceutical funding was used in the development or marketing of this book. Dr. Moira Rynn serves as the Chair of the Data Safety Monitoring Board for experimental compounds for pediatric behavioral health disorders for the following pharmaceutical companies: Abbvie, Inc. Katherine Ellison has nothing to disclose.

One final note before we get started. Depression, the focus of this book, is one of two varieties of mood disorders, the other of which is bipolar disorder. In bipolar disorder, depressed periods alternate with the sometimes giddy "highs" known as mania. If you're seeking information on that illness, please see our companion book, *If Your Adolescent Has Bipolar Disorder*.

Chapter One

Understanding Depression

If you've never suffered from depression, the first thing to know is that it's more serious than sadness. The illness affects both the brain and body, with emotional, mental, behavioral, and physical consequences. A single episode of untreated depression can last up to nine months, robbing a child of an entire school year.

Major depressive disorder is clinically defined as a pervasive feeling of sorrow, hopelessness, or apathy that lasts more than a couple weeks for a good part of each day; interferes with life at home, school, or work; and may not respond to changing circumstances. Some who have suffered depression would argue that even this description doesn't capture the pain.

Depression "is a wimp of a word" for a "howling darkness in the brain," the author William Styron wrote in his groundbreaking 1989 book, *Darkness Visible: A Memoir of Madness.*

"If I had to describe how depression made me feel in four words, I'd say *unwelcome in my mind*," writes Ruby Walker, in her self-published book: *Advice I Ignored: Stories and Wisdom from a Formerly Depressed Teen.* A few days before her 15th birthday, Walker had sunk so low that she stopped going to school for a full semester. "Day in, day out, I was bullying myself," she writes. "I was under constant attack."

An Illness (Almost) Like Any Other

Mood disorders, including depression, are in fundamental ways like any other illness. Hypertension affects the blood vessels; asthma affects the lungs; arthritis affects the joints; and mental illness affects the brain. Depression isn't due to bad character or lack of effort. You wouldn't urge a child with asthma to think positively the next time he or she has trouble breathing or one with diabetes to hope for the best the next time his or her blood sugar levels shoot up. Instead, you would surely try to provide the best possible professional treatment, while supporting your child at home. Plan on taking that same approach with your child's depression.

At the same time, there *are* some striking differences between mood disorders and purely physical illnesses. For one thing, we unfortunately still know much less about what causes mood disorders, although we do have some good ideas. Another big difference is the absence of any objective measuring technique—like a blood test or brain scan—to diagnose illnesses of the brain. Instead, a mental health professional or physician must evaluate a person's symptoms with the help of checklists and criteria provided in the *Diagnostic and Statistical Manual of Mental Disorders* (*DSM*), the regularly updated guide relied on by US mental health professionals. The latest version of this manual is a revision of the fifth edition, the *DSM-5*, released in 2022.

Adults and adolescents have similar symptoms, with a few variations. Experts note that depressed children, particularly boys, may often appear to be more irritable than sad, compared to their elders.

Below you'll see the key criteria for "major depressive disorder" from the *DSM-5*.

Diagnosing Depression

Five or more of the following symptoms must be present nearly every day during the same two-week period:

- Depressed or irritable mood for most of the day
- Markedly diminished interest or pleasure in almost all activities for most of the day
- Weight loss or weight gain or increase/decrease in appetite—or for children, failure to make normally expected weight gains
- Insomnia or hypersomnia (excessive sleeping)
- Fatigue or loss of energy
- Feelings of inappropriate guilt or hopelessness
- Indecisiveness or diminished ability to concentrate
- Recurrent thoughts of death or suicide, a suicide attempt or specific plan to do so
- Behavior that seems either overly keyed up or unnaturally slowed down

These symptoms must represent a marked change from the person's previous usual state; must impair functioning at home, work, or school; and cannot be due to the direct physiological effect of substance use or a medical condition. (This list was adapted from the American Psychiatric Association's *Diagnostic and Statistical Manual of Mental Disorders* [5th ed., text revision]. Arlington, VA: American Psychiatric Association, 2022.)

A Parent's Input

When diagnosing an adult, a therapist will glean most if not all information from talking directly to the patient. With adolescents, however, parents, guardians, and sometimes also teachers are important sources of information. Parents know their children's life histories better than anyone else. Parental input is key as well because the youth themselves may have trouble expressing their feelings, lack insight into them, or resist discussing them.

Red Flags

Depression doesn't usually appear full-blown overnight. Instead, it may start as anxiety, or a mild case of the blues that worsens over time. Often, the transition to a genuine disorder is so gradual that parents miss the warning signs until there is a crisis. As with any other illness, however, the earlier depression is professionally diagnosed and treated, the sooner suffering can be relieved, and the better the long-term outcome may be. That's why you should become familiar with these not-always-subtle behaviors, some of which are also clinical symptoms:

- Increased irritability: crankiness, hostility, or anger
- Decreased interest in friends and activities
- Difficulty concentrating
- A sudden drop in grades
- Frequent absences from school

- Complaints of tiredness, boredom, or vague aches and pains
- Changes in sleep patterns, such as insomnia or oversleeping
- Alcohol or substance use
- Social withdrawal
- Hypersensitivity to rejection or failure
- Self-deprecating remarks
- Thoughts that life is not worth living

Variations on a Theme

No two people get depressed in the same way.

A psychiatrist who diagnoses your child with depression may add a specifier that further describes what's going on. The list of these includes the following:

- *Chronic*—When symptoms of major depressive disorder last continuously for at least two years.
- *Catatonic*—When a depressed person's behavior seems either unnaturally slowed down or keyed up. This rare condition could include stupor, refusal to speak, purposeless overactivity, and peculiar mannerisms, such as grimacing or mimicking another person's speech or movements.
- *Melancholic*—Showing a near-complete lack of interest or pleasure in almost all activities. The person's mood never brightens, even temporarily, or when something good happens.
- *Psychotic*—When the depressed person suffers delusions—that is, beliefs out of touch with reality. This could include thinking other people can hear one's thoughts, or sensory perceptions of things that don't exist, such as disembodied voices.

- *Atypical*—More common than its name implies, especially in young people, this type of depression is diagnosed in people who can cheer up when something good happens before sinking back after it's over. Other symptoms may include significant weight gain, an increase in appetite, oversleeping, a weighed-down feeling in the arms or legs, and a long-running pattern of hypersensitivity to personal rejection.
- *Seasonal* (also known as seasonal affective disorder, or SAD)—When symptoms of depression start and stop around the same time each year. Typically, they begin in fall or winter and subside in spring. The onset seems to be linked directly to the change of season—in particular, reduced exposure to sunlight in winter—rather than the start of school, as some parents might assume.
- *Premenstrual*—Similar to premenstrual syndrome (PMS), but more serious in nature, premenstrual dysphoric disorder (PMDD) causes severe irritability, depression, or anxiety in the week or two before the start of a period, with symptoms usually going away two or three days afterward.

These are all varieties of major depressive disorder. There are also some related illnesses, which will be discussed in the following sections.

Persistent Depressive Disorder

Formerly known as "dysthymia," persistent depressive disorder has similar, though generally less severe, symptoms as major depression, may include irritability, and affects up to

8% of adolescents. The main difference is it's generally longer-lasting—with at least one year's duration for adolescents—meaning that even with its milder symptoms it may be more harmful, affecting children's educational and social learning.

Bipolar Disorder

In adolescents with bipolar disorder, depressed moods may alternate with manic or irritable "highs." (In contrast, major depressive disorder is sometimes referred to as "unipolar" depression.) This condition is much less common among both youth and adults than clinical depression, affecting fewer than 3% of US adolescents, yet is also more dangerous and harder to treat.

Bipolar disorder is often difficult to recognize early in life, yet the sooner it is identified, treated, and monitored, the better. One major warning sign is if your child goes through periods of appearing to need very little sleep. Adolescents with depression that does not improve over time, with psychotic symptoms such as hallucinations or unrealistic thinking, and with a family history of bipolar disorder are all at a higher risk for this disorder. Bipolar disorder requires a different treatment than depression, and it will include medications. For more information on bipolar disorder, please see our companion book, *If Your Adolescent Has Bipolar Disorder*.

Disruptive Mood Dysregulation Disorder

Disruptive mood dysregulation disorder (DMDD) describes a child who has an irritable or angry mood most of the day, nearly every day. Symptoms typically begin before age 10 and may include severe and otherwise inexplicable temper tantrums three or more times on average per week, together with trouble functioning at home or at school due to the irritable mood. To be diagnosed, a child must be under the age of 18 and have these symptoms steadily for 12 months or longer.

DMDD first became a diagnosis in 2013, with the publication of the *DSM-5*. It arose out of concerns that too many children with this problem were being misdiagnosed with bipolar disorder and possibly given the wrong medications. Today researchers believe that up to 5% of children and adolescents have this disorder. Yet the diagnosis remains controversial among experts who think normal childhood behavior is being overmedicalized. Some clinicians suggest that the explosive outbursts constitute more of a symptom, like a fever or sore throat, rather than a unique disorder. Still, researchers have found that while children diagnosed with DMDD may resemble children with bipolar disorder, more of them will go on to develop depression and anxiety.

Now, let's address some of the known and suspected causes of all these varieties of depressed mood.

What Are the Biological Roots of Depression?

Scientists have found clear evidence linking depression to a variety of physical phenomena, including individual differences in brain development and chemistry. It's worth the effort to familiarize yourself with some of these findings. A basic understanding of the physical aspects of depression can help you appreciate how at least some of your child's behavior is beyond his or her control. It may also make you more comfortable with a doctor's recommendation to use medication to treat a condition that has both medical and psychological components.

> "Once I learned a little bit about what lay behind my daughter's depression, I was more patient with her," says Jeanne, whose teen was hospitalized after a suicide attempt. "I also didn't get so stuck and frustrated when doctors tossed around words like 'serotonin' and 'cortisol.'"

Doctors may have your best interests at heart and still lapse into jargon or unnecessarily detailed clinical explanations when you are anxiously trying to make sense of a condition that they themselves don't completely understand, or about which the science remains unclear. Nor will many of them be able to give you satisfying answers during a typical office appointment during which they may be rushed and you may be feeling overwhelmed. You don't need a medical degree, however, to absorb the summary below. If you want to delve deeper, check out the Resources section at the end of this book, where among other things we recommend a couple of excellent lay-readers' books on the brain.

Variations in Brain Architecture

Researchers have found substantial evidence of measurable differences in the volume, thickness, and surface area of various brain regions of healthy children compared with those suffering from depression. The results of past studies aren't conclusive, however, and scientists today are hunting for clearer answers. Scientists working on several major longitudinal studies have been scanning young subjects' brains to examine the relationship between brain development over time and the expression of psychiatric disorders. While more research is needed, they have found evidence that certain brain structures are smaller in people with depression. Still unknown is whether that difference is causing the problem. In other words, are young people with smaller brain structures more likely to be depressed? Or has depression somehow already caused that difference? And are these changes permanent or reversible?

Note: If a clinician recommends that you have your child's brain scanned to diagnose a mental illness, we advise that you seek a second opinion, as this is not standard practice, may entail considerable expense, and is unlikely to be helpful. The exception to this rule is when neurological symptoms suggest another and possibly related medical illness.

Variations in Brain Chemistry

Another potentially significant difference in the brains of depressed people has to do with chemicals known as neurotransmitters. In healthy brains, these chemical messengers help the cells, called neurons, communicate with each other by ferrying messages across synapses, the gaps between cells. Yet in the brains of depressed people, something interferes with this process, causing changes in the balance of neurotransmitters that affect the way the neurons function. Until recently, scientists developing antidepressants have focused on serotonin, a neurotransmitter that helps regulate sleep, appetite, anxiety, and sexual drive. But today they understand that many more neurotransmitters are involved, including norepinephrine, dopamine, GABA (gamma-aminobutyric acid), and glutamate.

Norepinephrine influences the body's response to stress, and it helps regulate arousal, sleep, and blood pressure. Dopamine is essential for physical movement, while also influencing a person's sense of pleasure, motivation, and perception of reality. GABA plays a role in anxiety, and glutamate is key to overall brain functioning. Today's most popular antidepressant medications work by increasing the brain's supply of some of these neurotransmitters.

Again, scientists still need to figure out whether the chemical fluctuations they've found are the cause or effect of depression. Many believe the relationship cuts both ways, with brain chemistry affecting behavior, and behavior affecting brain chemistry. For instance, we know that stress can alter brain chemistry, leading to depression. Yet when people effectively manage their stress, they may be able to change their own brain chemistry and improve their moods.

Other Variations

Still another physical difference in people with depression involves the immune system. Increasing research has suggested that depression may be the result of chronic inflammation. This intriguing finding suggests there may be other important targets for treatment that researchers have yet to discover.

Lastly, and also promisingly, researchers are also looking at the guts. There's evidence that irritation in the gastrointestinal system signals the central nervous system in the brain and spinal cord, triggering mood changes. What if a microbiome transplant could help treat depression? Intriguing as this question may be, there is at this writing no systematic research to answer it.

As diagnostic technology, including brain scans, improves, there's new hope that scientists will soon better understand the causes of depression and other mood disorders, which could lead to many more effective treatments. We'll tell you more about the new research avenues in the Conclusion.

Does Gender Matter?

Gender is a factor in mood disorders of all kinds. Before puberty, the rates of depression are equal in boys and girls, but afterward, girls are two to three times as likely to have the disorder. We still have a lot to learn about why this is so, but researchers suspect it's partly due to the influence of hormones, and possibly also because girls are likelier to have suffered stressful events that contribute to the disorder. Gender may also help determine whether certain *types* of stress lead to depression. In one large recent study, female adolescents reported much more stress from peers ("mean girls") than did males.

Judging by one alarming statistic, the COVID-19 pandemic has been hardest on girls. Emergency room visits for suicide attempts rose 51% in 2021 for adolescent girls, compared with the same period in 2019. For boys, the rate rose by 4%.

At the same time, many young men with depression may simply express it differently, and therefore remain under the radar. Whereas depression—an "internalizing" disorder—appears more common among girls, other, more aggressive—"externalizing"—conditions, such as conduct problems and self-destructive substance use, are more common in boys.

As we've noted, depressed young men may seem less sad than irritable, as well as frustrated, risk-taking, and aggressive. Significantly, boys as a rule have been less likely than girls to seek help.

What About Race?

Some studies suggest that both African and Latino American youth experience more symptoms of depression than their white peers. Other research has found that African Americans suffer less acute episodes of depression than whites but are more likely to suffer from depression that is chronic and debilitating. Part of the problem is that racial minorities overall have been less likely to report problems and get care.

> Chamique Holdsclaw, a former women's professional basketball player, spent her early childhood with a father who suffered from schizophrenia and a mother who drank too much, neither of whom were getting treatment for their problems. At age 11 she was sent to live with her grandmother, who insisted that Holdsclaw see a social worker for her depression. "In our community, there's a strong feeling that you don't talk about these things, and that if anything you pray them away," she says. "But my grandmother was ahead of her time."

What Role Do Genes Play?

Depression doesn't have a single cause. Instead, it arises from the complex interplay of biological, social, and psychological factors. But researchers have found that one of the strongest factors in this mix is genetic. The offspring of depressed parents have a two to four times higher risk than those of non-depressed parents of developing the disease themselves. Such children are also more likely to develop depression at an early age and experience repeated episodes.

Despite this hereditary factor, many people with lots of relatives with depression never develop the disorder. Depression can also strike individuals with no family history. Children of depressed parents are most likely born with a genetic *predisposition* to depression, making them more vulnerable to environmental risk factors, such as various forms of stress.

The genetic component of depression means that many adolescents with the disorder may have one or two parents who share the illness, which itself can be a major source of stress. But relatives can also serve as positive role models, if they've managed to accept and learn to successfully treat their illness.

"I get depressed sometimes, just like Megan, and when I do, I've learned to step back, not work those 60-hour weeks, get outside, and get moving," says Jeanne. "I'm doing my best to teach her to figure out what helps her in those moments."

How Does Stress Affect Depression?

Stress is the body's natural response to a perceived threat—real or imagined, physical or psychological. In response to such alarms, the brain releases hormones that prepare the body to fight or flee. The heart rate, blood pressure, and muscle tension all increase. The rapid response system can save lives in a genuine emergency. Yet when stress is frequent or prolonged, it takes a toll on both the body and mind, sometimes leading to depression. In some children and adolescents, as in adults, scientists have found a strong link between depression and previous stressful life events. Recent studies have shown that a child's own genetic code may be changed by traumatic events, such as abuse, in what is known as an "epigenetic effect." This means adults who have had stressful early lives may be more likely to have children at risk for depression. Again, these outcomes are frequent but not universal. Some children who suffer stressful events never become depressed or pass on the risk of depression to their own kids.

Stress-induced depression isn't always traceable to a single trauma. It's often related to the cumulative impact of many incidents. Still, some major life events can raise the risk of the disorder. These include the loss of a parent through death, divorce, or other permanent separation, physical or emotional abuse, sexual assault, or bullying. Encouragingly, there are many ways parents can help increase resilience in their children, as we'll explain in more depth in Chapter 5.

Are You to Blame?

Many parents' greatest fear is that they caused their child's depression with less-than-perfect parenting.

> "When I think back to my son's early years, I know I made so many mistakes," says Beth. "I lost my temper—a lot. I wasn't home every evening for dinner. I didn't provide much structure and rules."

If you find yourself talking to yourself this way, keep in mind that many children who grow up under severe stress and even abuse never become depressed, while children raised by loving, attentive, competent parents can suffer from depression, just as they might develop other diseases.

> It wasn't until she serendipitously touched the scar under her daughter's sleeve that Charlene, a mother of three, discovered

that Ellen had been cutting her arms with a safety pin. After that, she noticed that Ellen was also skipping meals day after day. These were Charlene's first warning signs of Ellen's depression and eating disorder. "It was extraordinarily painful because I thought I could prevent that stuff by loving my body in front of my girls and never critiquing them," Charlene says. "Turns out nurture is often only a small part of the equation."

Depression, as we've explained, is a complex illness with multiple causes. Rest assured that garden-variety parenting mistakes won't create it in isolation. But it's also worth understanding how parents may influence a child's emotional development.

A warm, stable home makes a big difference in any young person's life. In contrast, chronic family conflict and an inconsistent or inattentive parenting style make it harder for children to learn how to form healthy, secure emotional attachments. Researchers have found that children of critical, rejecting, or controlling parents are more likely to develop a critical view of themselves and the world, leading to depression.

Of course, family dysfunction is a two-way street. Living with an adolescent can be challenging under the best of circumstances, yet when the child is exceptionally irritable, gloomy, or apathetic due to the depression, the difficulties increase exponentially. Families can get trapped in a vicious feedback loop, in which behavior related to depression creates conflict that increases depression and then causes even more conflict. Fortunately, appropriate treatment for the child's depression, which we detail in the next chapter, can help break the cycle.

Is Your Child's Personality a Factor?

"Temperament" is someone's inborn tendency to react to events in a particular way. As most parents know, such personality traits first become apparent in infancy or early childhood and tend to last throughout the lifespan. Temperament matters with depression. Some studies have found that young people who are shy, withdrawn, or easily upset are at increased risk of the disorder. So are born pessimists, who innately view the world as a threatening place and themselves as powerless to cope with many situations. Some people tend to blame themselves for negative events, even ones beyond their control. Temperament is largely hereditary, but it can be influenced by therapy.

"Comorbidities": The Extra Baggage

Up to nine in ten adolescents with depression have other emotional, behavioral, and learning problems, most commonly anxiety and attention-deficit/hyperactivity disorder (ADHD). As many as half will have two or more of them. These coexisting disorders—also known as "comorbidities"—will complicate your child's treatment plan, but it's essential to address them. Maybe your child's untreated ADHD, for example, is making him or her feel out of control and presenting a target for bullies, worsening or even causing the depression.

If you suspect your child has overlapping issues, you may want to seek out a neuropsychological workup, involving several hours of tests of cognitive and emotional abilities. The exam detects not only comorbidities but learning issues, such as dyslexia. Sometimes a school will pay to evaluate your child. If you can't get this kind of extensive testing, however, insist that the doctor diagnosing your child with depression is also checking for comorbidities.

Any one of the following coexisting conditions can aggravate depression and set back your child at school:

- *Anxiety*—More than 60% of depressed adolescents have experienced an anxiety disorder. It commonly begins before puberty, followed by major depression in adolescence. While all young people feel worried or nervous at times, an anxiety disorder can cause such overwhelming fear that it interferes with ability to function.

There are various types of anxiety disorders, including separation anxiety, which causes distress when the child is away from home or relatives; generalized anxiety, in which a child worries about *everything*, from schoolwork to the state of the world; and posttraumatic stress, in which someone is haunted by memories of a terrible event, such as a car accident or assault.

- *ADHD*—As many as one in ten US children have ADHD, of which the principal symptoms are distraction and impulsivity, and up to 38% of them also suffer from depression. ADHD symptoms may improve by late adolescence, but in most cases they last into adulthood.

Ruby Walker, who wrote a book about her depression as a teen, was diagnosed with ADHD four years after her first episode. Today she believes the ADHD was the underlying cause. Depression and anxiety are frequent fellow travelers with ADHD, especially for girls, who, like Ruby, more often slip under the radar, wait years before they're diagnosed, and can be extra-hard on themselves for making mistakes. "When I finally started meds for ADHD, it was a game-changer," she says.

- *Substance use disorder*—Self-destructive use of alcohol, tobacco, and recreational drugs is common in adolescents with depression. Alcohol itself can cause depressive symptoms, but sometimes a depressed child will turn to drinking or drug use to "self-medicate" and escape their emotional pain.
- *Eating disorders*—From one-third to one-half of all people with eating disorders also suffer from depression. Most are adolescent girls or young women. People with eating disorders may severely restrict what they eat, or binge-eat and then induce vomiting or misuse laxatives.
- *Oppositional defiant disorder (ODD)*—Most adolescents test the rules now and then, especially when tired, stressed, or upset. ODD is something more: defiant, uncooperative, and sometimes hostile behavior that can include angry outbursts, excessive arguing with adults, refusal to comply with requests, and deliberate attempts to annoy people.
- *Conduct disorder*—More severe than ODD, this disorder often includes criminal conduct. Children may threaten others, get into fights, set fires, vandalize property, lie, steal, stay out all night, or run away from home. Such youth are frequently labeled "bad" or delinquent rather than mentally ill, and some may wind up being written off as lost causes rather than getting the help they need.
- *Learning disorders*—Children with learning disorders, such as dyslexia and auditory processing disorder, are prone to being depressed. Depression itself can interfere with learning, robbing attention and motivation.
- *Gender dysphoria*—The *DSM-5* defines gender dysphoria as "a marked incongruence" between the gender a person

was born with and his or her experience, lasting at least six months, and associated with "clinically significant distress or impairment" socially or occupationally.

Parents often have trouble discerning whether a child's behavior is due to depression, another disorder, or garden-variety rebellion. An adolescent with dyslexia or ADHD may start skipping class, for instance, out of frustration with not being able to meet a teacher's demands. Or a child with anxiety may resist mingling with peers at recess. Defiance may be easier than acknowledging weakness. "I'd rather be bad than sad," is how one teenager with ADHD and depression frankly put it. Before you decide that your child is a troublemaker who needs to face strict consequences, consult a mental health professional to make sure the behavior isn't a plea for help.

For further information on the conditions described above, see the Resources section at the end of this book.

What's the Prognosis?

Depression may be more or less severe, depending on the child and other circumstances. But it most likely won't disappear overnight, and recovery will probably take time.

An untreated episode of major depression lasts an average of seven to nine months. After that, it's unfortunately likely that your child will have later episodes. One study found that more than 70% of teenagers who experienced a first episode of depression before age 18 had a second one within the next 12 years. After two episodes, the odds of a recurrence are even higher. Major depressive disorder is considered a chronic illness, but treatment can make a big difference. People who don't get treatment on average will suffer five to seven episodes of major depression, with each episode worsening over time.

The surprisingly good news is that depression is a lot more responsive to medical care and psychotherapy than many purely physical disorders, such as cancer and heart disease. Early treatment may help keep depression from becoming chronic or severe. It can also postpone or even prevent frequent recurrences, alleviate symptoms, and potentially prevent the greatest danger of the disorder, which is suicide.

If you think your adolescent may be suffering from depression, it's wise to seek professional help ASAP, even if your child says he or she doesn't want it or insists that nothing is wrong. You know what's normal and what's not for your child, so trust your instincts. At the very least, you may prevent needless emotional pain and suffering. At most, you may save a life.

In the next two chapters, we'll describe the kinds of help you may find.

Chapter Two

Treatment

Psychotherapy

If you're like many parents, having your child diagnosed with depression brings mixed feelings. You may be relieved to finally have an explanation for puzzling or even alarming behavior. But you may also reasonably wish it were something else—such as the flu or temporary stress from too much homework. There's this good news, however: You now have several promising paths to help your child get better.

We can't overstress the importance of educating yourself. You'll feel a lot more comfortable helping your child if you learn some of the basics and the right questions to ask. And please don't hesitate to ask questions. Each child is different, so you have a right to expect more than a formulaic treatment. What's more, each course of action has different risks and benefits. A good clinician will explain why one may be better than another.

If your child is showing only mild signs of sadness and no major changes in behavior, it's best to go slow, paying close attention and trying to reduce stress. But for anything more serious, this is the time to learn about the two most promising treatments for depression: psychotherapy, the formal term for "talk therapy," and medication.

> "Do everything you possibly can do to get the best care for your children," warns Bill, the father of a depressed adolescent. "You've got to fight as hard as you would if they'd fallen off a boat and you were trying to rescue them from drowning. It's that serious. The difference between good treatment, so-so treatment, and incompetent treatment can be a life-and-death issue with these kids."

Choosing Psychotherapy

Psychotherapy may require a major commitment of time, energy, and other resources. Yet it can greatly improve your child's outlook and teach coping skills that may last a lifetime.

Imaging studies have shown psychotherapy can lead to physical changes in the brain, just as medication does, although the kinds of changes observed are different. Rather than addressing the chemical nature of depression, psychotherapy targets the psychological, social, behavioral, and environmental aspects. Providers include psychiatrists, clinical psychologists, clinical social workers, mental health counselors, psychiatric nurses, and marriage and family therapists.

> In the second year of the pandemic, Brianna's 17-year-old daughter surprised her mother by announcing that she wanted to talk to a counselor. "I'd thought she was fine," Brianna said. "She's getting all A's and is into after-school sports; what's the problem?" But after a few weeks of twice-a-month appointments with a social worker, Brianna noticed a big difference. "She used to say a lot of doom-and-gloom stuff, like she had no friends and

would never get into college. Now I don't get that vibe anymore."

The Importance of Parental Health and Self-Care

Before we tell you more about psychotherapy for your child, here's a brief public service announcement about psychotherapy for *you.*

Self-care when you're coping with a struggling child is paramount for several reasons.

Remember that if your child has a mood disorder, you or your partner may likely have one, too. If that's the case, and you have yet to get treatment for yourself, now's a great time to do so. You'll not only be a good role model, but you won't be running this marathon with a heavy weight around your neck.

Psychotherapy helps you cope with the anger, sorrow, fear, and self-blame that can well up when you have a child in crisis. As much as you may worry about all sorts of worst-case scenarios, you can learn to be calm, and in doing so, you can help your child to be calmer as well.

Many parents who neglected their own self-care when they were younger find that having an ill child finally motivates them to seek help. This won't just improve your life but may help you avoid repeating the mistakes of your own parents, who themselves may have been suffering from depression. In other words: If you can find a way to afford the time and money—something we'll say more about later—this could be your chance to break a harmful generational cycle.

"I've struggled with depression, just like my daughter, but I've learned better ways to deal with it," says Janet.

"When I start to feel that way, it's time to spend more time with my dogs, be outside, go to yoga, and not work 60 hours a week. I've also learned that it's okay to take a time out to process information, which is how you make better decisions."

What Psychotherapies May Be Best for My Child?

Several kinds of psychotherapy are used to treat depression, either alone or in a combination. One of the best-studied approaches is *cognitive-behavioral therapy* (CBT). A therapist using CBT challenges a patient's unhealthy thinking patterns, asking questions that can reveal misassumptions and unrealistic pessimism, while encouraging problem-solving skills, healthier choices, and a more positive worldview. Studies suggest there can be benefits after even just five sessions.

In a typical conversation, a therapist might push back when a patient insists she has no friends who truly care for her.

"What makes you think that?" the therapist might ask.

"I texted one of my friends yesterday and she took a whole day to answer," the patient may say.

The interchange highlights the way that many depressed adolescents may distort reality. They may draw conclusions based on limited or no information (the friend may have had an emergency). Or they may magnify the importance of a single event to make general and incorrect assumptions. The therapist can help the patient keep in mind information that refutes a dire view of the world and help identify the positives she's overlooking—such as the fact that the friend did eventually text back.

This is also known as "reframing."

In another example, if your child says something like "I'm so stupid! I always blurt out ridiculous things when I'm talking to friends," the therapist might gently call attention to his or her habit of negative self-talk and encourage ways to see the behavior in another light, such as the way some mistakes can be learning opportunities and are simply part of growing up.

CBT can help depressed adolescents:

- Monitor moods
- Think more positively
- Schedule pleasant activities
- Set and achieve goals
- Cope with social situations
- Relax and manage stress
- Solve many everyday problems

Another popular and well-studied approach to treat depression is *interpersonal psychotherapy* (IPT), which, just like it sounds, focuses on interpersonal issues as triggers for the illness. This may be useful if your son or daughter is constantly getting into conflicts with you or others, lacks social skills, or is grieving over a recent loss. It's also helpful during a stressful transition, such as changing schools or coping with one's parents' divorce. IPT works to identify the problem that triggered the episode of depression and develop the social and communication skills needed to resolve it.

IPT can help adolescents with depression learn to handle social issues such as:

- Establishing independence
- Dealing with peer pressure
- Forming healthy friendships
- Resolving family conflicts

Either CBT or IPT may be used in individual therapy, in which your child works one on one with a therapist, or in a therapist-led group. Group therapy gives kids with depression a chance to discuss their concerns and trade insights with peers struggling with similar issues, while reminding them that they are not alone. The group setting also offers adolescents a chance to learn and practice social skills. The relationships formed in the group can be a powerful antidote to feelings of helplessness and hopelessness.

Dialectical behavior therapy (DBT), a therapy often used with depressed adolescents, employs mindfulness principles—teaching how to be more present in the moment—and skill-building to help manage stress and improve relationships. The full program consists of several sessions of both group and one-on-one therapy, each once a week, with phone coaching available between sessions.

By giving kids techniques to better tolerate emotional distress, DBT can help discourage self-destructive actions, which might range from blurting out an insult to a teacher or boss to attempting suicide. One common technique is "chain analysis," which tries to show how unwanted behaviors may result from a chain of interrelated events. The therapist coaxes the patient to think back to what may have been the first, precipitating "link" in that chain: perhaps a bad night's sleep, harmful use of drugs or alcohol, or intense emotions caused by something someone else said or did. Once the patient recognizes the sequence, the therapist can help brainstorm about ways to help prevent it from being repeated, including by coming up with healthier responses. Some therapists work with youth to create a list of pleasurable distracting activities such as reaching out to a trusted friend or family member, going for a walk, or working out at the gym.

Who Is Most Likely to Be Helped by Psychotherapy?

Psychotherapy alone may go far to help adolescents who are mildly or moderately depressed. If the illness is severe, however, you may want to try medication as well. For the best results, your adolescent should be open to and willing to speak with a therapist. In CBT and sometimes in other types of psychotherapy, the therapist may assign homework, such as keeping a journal or practicing new skills. To get the most out of the process, it is important for the therapist to engage and help the child try this work.

"I don't see the fact that I never went to therapy until literally last year as some kind of point of pride," says Ruby Walker, who waited four years after her first bout with depression to see a college counselor. "I see it as a sad mistake. Professionals know what they're doing. I wish I hadn't tried to work everything out myself. It's okay to need help."

Are There Any Downsides to Psychotherapy?

Psychotherapy may have fewer adverse impacts than medication, but it's not risk-free. It is meant to tap into deep, sometimes disturbing, thoughts and feelings, so any therapist you choose should be prepared to handle unexpected strong reactions. Starting therapy could lead your child to feel worse temporarily. Assuming you trust the therapist, and he or she is offering a well-regarded treatment, you'll want to encourage your child to hang in there and work through those feelings.

If your adolescent is taking medication, the therapist should be knowledgeable about the effects and willing to coordinate treatment with your child's psychiatrist or another prescriber. If your child has other mental, emotional, or behavioral disorders in addition to depression, the therapist should be well-versed in these conditions as well.

On top of these concerns are some obvious potential problems. You should make sure your child's therapist is credentialed, experienced, and ethical. (We will advise you how to do this in Chapter 4.)

Sometimes therapy is ineffective, resulting in wasted time and money and potentially worsening of the illness. Therapists are like any other profession—there are great ones, not-so-great ones, and those who should be avoided at all costs.

Therapists who violate young people's boundaries—whether physical or emotional—are fortunately rare yet can do deep and lasting harm. Tempting as it may be, avoid engaging a therapist who is already a friend of anyone in the family. Keep an eye on the relationship and be aware that psychotherapy should not involve physical contact other than a pat on the shoulder or handshake.

How Long Should My Child Be in Therapy?

The number of sessions needed for a particular adolescent depends on many factors, including the nature and severity of the symptoms. Unfortunately, the amount of time your child spends in therapy may also be dictated by the terms of your insurance coverage. Initially, psychotherapy sessions may be scheduled weekly. But as your child starts to feel better, the sessions may gradually be spaced farther apart. Even after your child's symptoms have improved, it's often helpful to continue those less-frequent sessions for several months. Continuing psychotherapy gives kids and families a chance to keep practicing new skills and to be more attuned to the thoughts and behaviors that might otherwise contribute to a relapse.

At some point during the first few sessions, your adolescent and the therapist may together create a list of short-term and long-term goals. It's a good idea to revisit this list periodically with your child and the therapist to gauge progress. Yet it's essential to give psychotherapy enough time to work. Don't expect lasting benefits overnight. At the same time, it's reasonable to expect gradual but noticeable progress over time. Don't hesitate to ask the therapist for an idea of how soon your child is likely to start noticing improvement and how long therapy is expected to last. If the therapy is taking much longer than planned, feel free to ask the therapist why. If you get an evasive or unsatisfactory answer, you should consider seeking a second opinion, just as you would for any other illness.

Private Lives

Study after study has shown that by far the most important factor determining success in psychotherapy is the bond between the patient and the therapist. As the person paying the bills and dragging your child to the sessions, you may reasonably want to participate in the actual process behind the therapist's closed doors, or at least be in on some of the secrets being revealed. You may also be desperately worried about your child's safety and anxious to know what you can do to help.

There are some ways that parents will need to be involved in an adolescent child's therapy. This includes providing information during the initial assessment, after which some therapists will have a first session jointly with the parent and child. During this process, the therapist should establish a plan. Most will make time to update the parent every several weeks or so. The manuals for CBT and IPT include parent sessions as part of the treatment plan. Beyond that, bear in mind that your child may not get the best results if he or she suspects the therapist is routinely spilling secrets to you. You may help your child most by respecting this important new relationship.

An exception to this rule is if your child is in danger of harm or harming others—from being abused to experimenting with dangerous drugs. In that case, the provider is obliged to act, which may include letting you know or even calling the police.

Here's something else to keep in mind as your child begins treatment. The 21st Century Cures Act, signed into law in 2016, requires providers to make their medical notes accessible to their patients. Most adolescents starting at age 12 (this varies depending on the state) will therefore be able to read their medical records, including the therapist's notes, online, and have the option to let their parents read them as well. Some research suggests that this transparency improves communication and satisfaction with treatment. Yet it can also raise problems, including with patients' reactions. It is one thing for someone to reveal secrets in private, but seeing the personal details or therapist's opinions in writing can be disturbing. You and your adolescent should talk to your provider to understand how he or she might document sensitive information.

As your son or daughter's therapy progresses, pay special attention to the quality of the relationship between your child and the therapist, as that will make all the difference as to whether it succeeds. You may have a few false starts before you find someone truly effective.

"No matter what, do not settle!" says Lisa Himmel, who cowrote a book with her mother, Sheila, about her eating disorder and depression as an adolescent. "I cannot emphasize enough the importance of truly connecting with the professional. I actually had a therapist in college who was terrible, two in fact, but I went for too long. On the other hand, there's often a level of resistance with the initial stages of therapy, so you do need to be sure to give the person at least a few sessions before concluding to continue or terminate."

What's the Bottom Line on Psychotherapy for Depression?

As an initial treatment for mild or moderate depression, psychotherapy can help adolescents develop important coping strategies. It can also help families manage the conflict that often accompanies the illness. The likelihood that depression will recur after the therapy is higher for adolescents who start out with more severe symptoms or who come from families with serious conflict. In such cases, adding medication may be especially helpful.

Chapter Three

Treatment

Medication

Antidepressants have helped many millions of children, adolescents, and adults ward off depression, which is why they are such a key part of conventional treatment. As of this writing, nearly one in seven US adults takes an antidepressant medication. Yet studies indicate that up to 30% of people with depression can't tolerate antidepressants or don't respond to them.

Medication is clearly not a panacea for treating depression, for adults or adolescents. Parents deliberating about whether to try them also have several other good reasons for caution. All medications come with side-effects, as we'll describe in more detail below. More broadly, you may reasonably distrust pharmaceutical firms' hard sell to consumers on TV and other media—something they're only legally allowed to do in the United States and New Zealand. Maybe you're also aware that the safety and efficacy of psychotropic medications—drugs affecting the brain—have been studied much more in adults than in children or adolescents, whose brains are still developing. For all these reasons and more, trying medication with your child can be a lonely and difficult decision. You may feel you have to sort through conflicting information, including misinformation and hype from passionate critics and proponents. Our advice is that despite the many caveats, it's worth giving medication a try if you find yourself in a crisis, or if your child isn't responding to psychotherapy.

> "In the beginning I was like, 'Meds? Not for my family!'" says Charlene, whose 15-year-old daughter tried to kill herself by jumping off a roof. "Now I'm like 'What else you got?' I didn't know we needed them 'til we needed them."

What Medications Help Depression in Kids?

Medications to treat depression are—no surprise—known as antidepressants. The front-line treatment for youth with depression and anxiety is a group known as selective serotonin reuptake inhibitors (SSRIs). Remember serotonin? SSRIs increase the level of serotonin in the brain by targeting a process known as "reuptake," in which neurotransmitters are reabsorbed by a cell in a way that can reduce their effect. The SSRIs allow a steadier supply of the chemical, which can decrease symptoms of depression. At this writing, after extensive tests for safety and efficacy, the US Food and Drug Administration (FDA) has approved only two SSRIs for treatment of major depressive disorder in children and teens. They are fluoxetine, with the famous brand name Prozac, approved for ages 8 and older, and escitalopram, or Lexapro, approved for ages 12 and older.

The Trials of Trial and Error

Even after all that testing, these medications won't work for every child, and sometimes they'll have intolerable side-effects. Your child's doctor may need to try a few different approaches before figuring out the best medication and dose. This requires patience and faith on all sides.

You'll want to give a medication the best chance to succeed by working with the prescriber over up to three months, at the start, to figure out whether it can be effective, and if so, at what optimum dose. The clinician should always start with the minimally effective dose, increasing it if needed, depending on your adolescent's response, up to the maximum advisable limit before trying a different formula. If side-effects are a problem, the clinician may try reducing the dose before switching to another medication.

You can support this process by keeping notes on any changes in your child's mood and behavior during the medication trials. Consider keeping a journal, or if you want to get techy, there's an app (actually several apps) for that. We provide some options in the Resources section, but you can also easily track one down by googling "mood" and "app." Make sure to check the price before you buy, because you don't need to spend a lot of money for this. It might be more than enough to note a few basic variables, such as changes in sleep habits, appetite, focus, and, of course, mood.

What Are Possible Side-Effects?

Side-effects are common irritants with any new medication, but here's the rub about antidepressants: While their side-effects appear right away—and then, often, subside—the benefits normally don't kick in for more than a month. This can be a major obstacle when you're trying to persuade your child to stick to a new regimen.

The most common side-effects of SSRIs are stomach upsets, including nausea and diarrhea, daytime sleepiness, vivid dreams, and headaches. Sometimes your child will become more agitated and impulsive. One frequent effect is a change in sexual function: decreased libido and reduced capacity to achieve orgasm. This is something few adolescents will want to tell their parents, but which may guarantee they stop taking the pills.

An uncommon but serious risk of taking SSRIs is "serotonin syndrome," the symptoms of which may include high blood pressure and a fast heart rate, and which in rare cases requires hospitalization.

> "You need to understand how important you are to the process," warns the father of a depressed son. "The psychiatrist isn't there with your child 24/7. He's not seeing the effects of the meds. Don't be afraid to call him back if you see anything that doesn't make sense to you."

Another rare but potentially serious risk is that antidepressants may trigger mania in kids who have bipolar disorder but have not yet had a first episode. Before prescribing an antidepressant, your child's doctor should carefully review your family history to see if anyone has been diagnosed with bipolar disorder and should always warn parents about the possibility of "switching"—the rapid transition from depression to mania. Unfortunately, some don't ask, so if you know there is a history of bipolar disorder in your family and you're not asked about it, speak up!

Coping With Side-Effects

Don't hesitate to call the doctor or go to a hospital emergency department if you or your child notice any serious symptoms, especially high fever, extreme dizziness, blood in stools, loss of consciousness, seizures, or suicidal behavior. (The bright side is that all of these are quite rare.) Most side-effects are easily managed. Reducing the dose may be enough, but here are a couple other strategies to discuss with the doctor:

- *Mix it up.* Taking the pill at night can help with daytime sleepiness, and taking it with meals can relieve nausea.
- *Prevent interactions.* Make sure your child is not drinking alcohol while taking antidepressants, as it can reduce the benefits and in some cases worsen side-effects. Marijuana and CBD may also reduce the effectiveness and increase side-effects. Check with your doctor or pharmacist before your child takes any over-the-counter or other prescription drugs. Even some cough syrups can be dangerous while taking SSRIs.

One more note about side-effects. The trial-and-error process of finding the right antidepressant, with the fewest untoward effects, has been so frustrating that many patients and doctors alike have been looking for workarounds. Your clinician may suggest that your child take a DNA test purportedly to find the best medication as soon as possible. Some patients and doctors swear by this method, despite its steep out-of-pocket cost.

"We found that my daughter couldn't tolerate benzos, which saved us from a possible disaster," says Julie.

As of this writing, however, both the FDA and the American Psychiatric Association say these tests have no proven value and shouldn't be ordered.

Do Antidepressants Increase the Risk of Suicide?

Of all the potential side-effects of SSRIs, the most worrisome is their well-publicized association with suicidal thoughts and behavior, known as suicidality. (This can include planning and attempting suicide.)

In 2004, after reviewing research involving more than 4,400 young people with major depression and other mental disorders, the FDA found a slightly increased risk of suicidality in young people up to the age of 25 during the first few months of treatment with antidepressants. (The average risk of such thoughts and behavior was 4% in young people taking an antidepressant, compared to 2% in young people taking a placebo.)

The FDA consequently required manufacturers of all antidepressant drugs to put strongly worded advisories—a "black box" warning—on their labeling. Pharmacists must also hand out written material about the risks to patients and families.

This warning is challenging to understand because it's so difficult to untangle the relationship between antidepressant treatment and the development of suicidality, which is already a common symptom of depression. It's worth keeping in mind that the rise in SSRI use has coincided with a *net fall* in suicide rates among adolescents. Our opinion is that on balance, and with careful support, these medications save lives.

The FDA Warning—Summarized

- Antidepressants increase the risk of suicidal thinking and behavior (suicidality) in children, adolescents, and young adults with major depression and other mental disorders.
- Health care professionals considering the use of an antidepressant in a child or adolescent for any clinical purpose must balance the risk of increased suicidality with the clinical need.
- Patients starting therapy should be observed closely for clinical worsening, suicidality, or unusual changes in behavior.
- Families and caregivers should be advised to closely observe the patient and to communicate with the prescriber.

Red Flags

If your child has started taking an SSRI, let the doctor know promptly if these symptoms develop or grow worse:

- Anxiety
- Panic attacks
- Worsening depression
- Agitation
- Irritability
- Hostility
- Impulsivity
- Extreme restlessness
- Rapid speech
- Insomnia
- Self-injurious behavior
- Suicidal thoughts

No One Said This Would Be Easy

Again, the decision to try medication for a child is never simple for parents. Sometimes it feels downright traumatic. Even as serious side-effects are rare, just knowing that they're possible is unsettling, to say the least. A prescription also confirms that there is truly a serious problem. Antidepressants carry much more stigma than, say, blood pressure medication. But in some cases they can be just as life-saving.

> Joaquin and Maria knew they had to take strong measures after their daughter Lourdes, at 12, stopped wanting to go to school, stopped talking to them, and began cutting her legs with a safety pin. Still, deciding to give her Prozac was "like jumping off a cliff for us," says Joaquin.
>
> As first-generation Puerto Ricans, the couple had to overcome an extra measure of judgment from friends and family. "In our culture, seeking mental health help of any kind is very much a taboo," says Maria. "Taking medications categorizes individuals as insane, broken." Maria and Joaquin took the plunge despite their upbringing, and today are glad they did. "The medication was actually the best decision we made," Maria says.

How Long Will My Child Need Medication?

The treatment of depression has three phases, each with its own goal. In the initial, "acute" phase, to use clinicians' jargon, the goal is for the patient to return to the level of functioning that existed before the illness. The next phase, "continuation," aims to prevent a relapse—the re-emergence of symptoms. Finally, in the "maintenance" phase, you may want to continue treatment for some time to prevent another episode of depression. The trickiest part of all this is that when people taking medication begin to feel better, they often want to quit.

The American Academy of Child and Adolescent Psychiatry (AACAP) recommends that after an initial depressive episode, patients should stay on medication for at least six if not a full twelve months after the symptoms have improved by 50%. (This would be added to whatever time it takes to find an effective formula and dose of antidepressant.) For those who have already experienced two or more depressive episodes, a doctor may recommend an even longer period.

A Spoonful of Sugar

No medicine will work if it doesn't go down the hatch. Yet unfortunately, many adolescents refuse or forget to take their pills as prescribed, even for illnesses such as asthma, for which there isn't nearly the same degree of stigma.

Your child's success with medication will depend on many factors, not least of which will be the strength of the relationship with the prescribing doctor and your ability to communicate faith in the benefits. We recommend that you not expect your child to be responsible for filling his or her own prescriptions—for now, at least, you've got to take that on. Also, to the best of your ability, respect your child's need for privacy and support his or her decision about sharing treatment information in other settings, such as summer camp, sleepovers, and visits to relatives.

Below are other tips from parents who've figured out ways to encourage good medication habits:

- Speak honestly about the pros and cons of medication treatment—adolescents usually sense when they're not getting the full story. But once you and your child decide to go forward, don't dwell on your misgivings:

  "Once we made the decision to try medication, for some very good reasons, I knew we had to put our worries aside and reflect our hopefulness that this would make a difference," says Beth. "Our son didn't need to know how difficult a decision it was for us."

- Take responsibility for storing and supervising the medication for a child under 18:

  "In our home, it's just known that everyone takes their medication, including me," says Vanessa. "I'm in charge of setting out all our medications at night. I put them in those little seven-day pillboxes, so we can see at a glance if anyone forgot to take their medication today."

- Figure out what your child wants and speak to that:

  "I recommend doing 'motivational interviewing,'" says Sally. "My goals simply aren't as meaningful to Larry as his goals are to him. So I've gotten to know the ways he thinks the medications might help him—like getting better at the guitar—and talk about that, rather than talking about his doing better in school or whatever I'm worried about."

- Set clear expectations for older adolescents who are still living at home:

  "We've talked a lot with Jerry about how his illness can affect everyone else in the house, and how taking his medications makes it easier on all of us," says Jerry's father, Roy.

Tapering Off

When it's time to stop the medication, your child's doctor will likely advise you to reduce the dose gradually over several weeks. This is to avoid discontinuation symptoms, which can be uncomfortable but aren't medically dangerous. Don't make this decision during a time of unusual stress. This may also be a good time to start or continue with psychotherapy.

Patients who discontinue medication too quickly can experience flu-like symptoms, dizziness, and sleep changes, and some return to depression, emerging within days to weeks of stopping the medication or lowering the dose. Some patients have also reported strange sensations such as a ringing in the ears or "zaps" that seem like electrical charges.

The bright side is that the symptoms of discontinuation are usually temporary and tapering helps. (A Harvard Medical School study of adults found that patients who reduced their dose over two or more weeks were less likely than those who stopped cold turkey to experience a relapse of depression.)

Discontinuation symptoms don't mean your child is "addicted"—that is, craving the drug—but do suggest that your child's brain has experienced a biological change. This also means that they'll disappear quickly if your child resumes the medication. You're not going to have to wait weeks as you did when the drug was first taking effect.

Some Questions for Your Child's Doctor

When medication is part of your child's treatment plan, be sure to tell the doctor about any other prescribed or over-the-counter drugs or herbal supplements your child is taking, since some of these may interact in harmful ways. Also tell the doctor if your child has allergies to any drug. Then make sure you have all the facts you need about any new medication prescribed. Here are some questions for which you'll need answers:

- When and how often should my child take the medication?
- How do you suggest we monitor how my child is doing with this new medication?
- Have studies been conducted using this medication in children?
- Should the medicine be taken with food or on an empty stomach?
- When should we expect to see results?
- What are the possible side-effects, and which are the most serious?
- What should I do if these side-effects occur?
- What number should I call if there's an emergency, or if I have questions or concerns?
- How long should my child stay on the medication?
- What if we want to stop the medication or reduce the dose?
- Will my child need to limit any activities while taking the drug?
- Does the medication interact with alcohol, other drugs, or certain foods?
- Where can I get more information on the medication?

What's the Bottom Line on Antidepressants?

Any adolescent who is taking an antidepressant should be under the care of a clinician with expertise in psychiatric medications, whether that's a pediatrician, nurse practitioner, or psychiatrist. Pay special attention to the first weeks after your child starts the medication, as this is when side-effects are most likely to appear.

Don't expect a dramatic turnaround in your child's mood. If your child isn't feeling any better after two to six weeks, the doctor may try increasing the dose up to the allowable maximum level. If that doesn't help, it may be necessary to try a different medication or add a second one. Since there is no way to know in advance how a particular person will react to a given antidepressant, some trial and error may be required to find the best medication and dose. Try to be patient and encourage your child to take the time needed.

What If My Child Doesn't Respond to First-Line Treatments?

Remember, up to 30% of people with depression don't respond to standard antidepressants or can't tolerate the side-effects. Moreover, in some unfortunate cases, an SSRI will simply stop working, a phenomenon colorfully known as "Prozac poop-out." It's of course important to make sure the child has actually been taking the pills. Sometimes the problem is simply poor communication.

A young person may stop taking a medication without letting anyone know due to reasons that could include side-effects, lack of a sense of benefit, social pressure, and concerns about long-term effects. This may require changes to the treatment plan, such as modifying or adding psychotherapy. If the adolescent is still suffering, a clinician may add or substitute other medications which haven't been FDA-approved for adolescent depression. This practice is known as prescribing "off-label."

What Is "Off-Label"?

Off-label means that a medication hasn't been FDA-approved for a specific illness or age group. While it may sound sketchy, it's a common practice that many prescribers have found to be safe and effective. And fortunately, insurance companies often will cover an off-label prescription if a first-line, approved medication has been tried without success.

An off-label prescription could simply mean using a medication approved for adults but not for adolescents, which is often simply because the appropriate studies haven't yet been done. For instance, sertraline (Zoloft) is approved to treat depression in adults but not in adolescents. Yet it *has* been approved to treat obsessive-compulsive disorder in adolescents, which means adolescents can take it safely, and many prescribers have found it can help adolescents with depression. Some clinicians will also try medications that are FDA-approved to treat depression in adults but have not been tested on adolescents for any illness. We provide a list of medications and their FDA approval status in the Appendix.

Non-SSRIs

Your child's clinician may want to try one of a group of antidepressants that target neurotransmitters other than serotonin—most commonly norepinephrine. Venlafaxine (Effexor), duloxetine (Cymbalta), and more recently levomilnacipran (Fetzima) can increase the activity of both serotonin and norepinephrine. Other popular antidepressants are bupropion (Wellbutrin), which increases the activity of serotonin, norepinephrine and dopamine, and mirtazapine (Remeron), which targets norepinephrine and serotonin. Sometimes a doctor will combine two of these medications. (In very rare cases, a clinician may decide a different approach is needed and prescribe an antipsychotic medication or a mood stabilizer.)

Each of the newer antidepressants has its own set of side-effects. Some are similar to those accompanying the SSRIs. Wellbutrin, for instance, may increase anxiety and in rare cases, in high doses or combined with other antidepressants or alcohol, can cause seizures.

If your child's doctor suggests trying an older medication, such as tricyclic antidepressants (including imipramine and amitriptyline) or monoamine oxidase inhibitors (MAOIs), such as phenelzine (Nardil) and tranylcypromine (Parnate), you should question the choice, as these have not only not been proven to be effective in adolescents but have more serious side-effects than SSRIs.

Plan B

Neuromodulation

If no conventional or even unconventional medication has worked, you may still have options to treat severe depression in your child. The first two we'll describe constitute an approach known as "neuromodulation": techniques that aim to change brain functioning with different kinds of stimulation. At this writing, these methods are only very rarely used for adolescents, and only if the illness is extremely serious and resistant to other treatments.

Electroconvulsive therapy (ECT) employs electrodes positioned on the scalp that deliver a carefully controlled electrical current to the brain, producing a seizure that may last about a minute. ECT can seem scary, especially if you watched Jack Nicholson receiving the treatment in *One Flew Over the Cuckoo's Nest*. But it is generally safe and sometimes quite effective, helping to explain why the AACAP says ECT may be used with adolescents with severe mood disorders after at least two medications have failed or in a crisis when there isn't time to wait for medication to work. The conditions for its use—including the age of the patient and whether or how many experts must approve it—vary from state to state, and the treatment isn't always accessible.

> "It gave me the creeps when I first heard it, but ECT was the one treatment that turned my daughter around," says Miles, the father who discovered his teenaged daughter Jenny had been cutting her skin. "The treatments made her very tired but over time helped stop her from hurting herself."

ECT temporarily changes the brain's electrochemistry. Before treatment, patients receive a muscle relaxant, to prevent the body from convulsing, and general anesthesia. They awaken a few minutes later, as if having had minor surgery. It typically requires 6 to 12 treatments, administered three times a week. The effects appear gradually over the course of the treatment. The most common side-effects are headache, aching muscles, nausea, and confusion. These usually occur within hours of a treatment and clear up quickly. Yet as the treatments go on, people also may have trouble remembering newly learned information, and some have partial and short-term loss of memories from the days, weeks, or months preceding the treatment. On the other hand, some people report that their memory improves after ECT, since their mind is no longer operating in a fog of depression.

The second neuromodulation technique, *transcranial magnetic stimulation* (TMS), has recently been getting rave reviews in the media, although the basic procedure has been studied since 1995. The FDA has approved TMS for medication-resistant depression in adults. It is still considered experimental in the treatment of adolescents.

In TMS, an electromagnetic coil is placed against the scalp, near the forehead. It delivers a pulse that stimulates cells in parts of the brain that may have reduced activity when someone is depressed. An advantage of this treatment is that it doesn't require surgery, hospitalization, or anesthesia. Typically, 30-minute sessions are given five days a week over two to four weeks.

In studies to date, the side-effects have been relatively mild and infrequent. They include discomfort, headache, or light-headedness during treatment, all of which usually go away soon after the session ends. Yet there is also a risk that the treatment might trigger a seizure.

A big caveat here: At this writing, only one large study has examined the treatment of depressed adolescents with TMS compared to a placebo approach. The study, which was industry-sponsored, found no difference in outcomes between the two groups—that is, no perceptible benefit. More research is obviously needed to determine if TMS can help this age group. Based on what we know today, we don't recommend it unless and until future studies show it is safe and effective.

Ketamine

Unless you've been on a long news fast, you've probably heard about a lot of new excitement about various psychedelic drugs, including LSD, psilocybin mushrooms, and MDMA—also known as "Ecstasy"—to treat severe depression and related illnesses. Major universities, including Yale, Johns Hopkins, and the University of California at Berkeley, have set up centers to study psychedelic therapies for all sorts of psychiatric illnesses, and investors are pouring funds into startups to market them.

At this writing, the only psychedelic that a doctor may legally prescribe for treatment-resistant depression is ketamine, a drug that got its start several decades ago as an anesthesia for animals, and was later used to help treat injured soldiers in Vietnam. It has also been used recreationally: injected, smoked or snorted, with names like Special K and Vitamin K.

In 2019, the FDA approved Spravato (the brand name for esketamine, a more potent form of ketamine) nasal spray to treat adult depression for patients who hadn't been helped by other medications. Two years later, the first, small study of adolescents (a group of 17, aged 13 to 17) found ketamine to be well-tolerated and effective in reducing symptoms of depression, at least in the short term, when compared to a placebo. For these reasons, some psychiatrists have called for urgent additional research of this option for children in crisis.

Unlike standard antidepressants, which target serotonin, norepinephrine, and dopamine, ketamine acts on glutamate. It can cause feelings of euphoria, unreality, and sensory distortions, lasting about two hours.

Paola's son Martin was 18 when his grandmother died and Martin became so depressed that he couldn't get out of bed. On the advice of his doctor, Paola brought him to a clinic for a series of six infusions of ketamine. "Martin has ADHD, so these were like trips to the funhouse for him; he was very into it," Paola says of her son. The sessions, which weren't covered by insurance, cost more than $3,000 altogether, but for several months it seemed the cloud had lifted. "The problem with ketamine is it doesn't last," Paola says. She suspects the benefits may have taken hold and lasted longer had a therapist been involved to help her son integrate the experience. She may try again in the future but says that for now, "We're back to where we were before the sessions."

Be advised that recreational use of ketamine is not therapeutic and carries risks including high blood pressure and dangerously slowed breathing. Ketamine should only be used in controlled settings, such as at a doctor's office, where a patient is closely watched for the two hours or so of the experience. Patients typically get the nasal spray twice a week for one to four weeks, then once a week for the next two months or so, and then once every week or two after that. Some patients will later need boosters.

The spray carries an FDA warning about side-effects, including sedation and trouble with attention, judgment, and thinking, as well as the risk for abuse or misuse of the drug and suicidal thoughts and behaviors. In some cases it has triggered psychosis, and it can also be fatal for people who abuse alcohol. For all of these reasons, despite the hoopla, we can't—at least not at this writing—vouch for ketamine use with adolescents.

What Are Some Promising Additional Tools?

Light therapy—also called phototherapy—may help treat seasonal affective disorder (SAD).

Although the biological mechanisms that cause SAD are still unknown, it's thought they may have to do with the way light exposure affects the brain's production of melatonin, a hormone that regulates the body's internal clock. Another theory suggests that light may alter the activity of certain neurotransmitters involved in depression, such as serotonin and dopamine.

Whatever the explanation, research on adults suggests exposure to intense artificial light may help relieve the symptoms of SAD. What's more, this is a relatively inexpensive, DIY treatment that can supplement other therapies. You can buy a special fluorescent desk lamp (providing full-spectrum light, similar to sunlight), enclosed in a protective box, online for as little as $40. Make sure it specifies at least 5,000 K (Kelvin). (It's a great going-away gift to teenagers heading for college.) Your child sits in front of the light for 30 to 60 minutes per day, ideally in the morning, avoiding staring directly at the light. Most people who respond to the light start to improve in a week or less, but some need several weeks to feel the full effects. Possible side-effects include eyestrain, headache, irritability, and insomnia. Light therapy is also not a good idea for those with a history or high risk of bipolar disorder, since it can potentially trigger a manic state.

> Light therapy did wonders for Allie, according to her mother, who says: "Allie is very verbal, and she used to say things like, 'Just look at all this gray. I can feel myself getting depressed.' So her psychiatrist prescribed a light box, and it seemed to lift her mood. The cat and dog would come sit by her because they liked the light. I think it improved the cat's mood, too!"

Do Any Dietary Supplements Help Depression?

Plenty of nutritional supplements are advertised as being able to improve mood. Still, keep in mind that if supplements did everything their manufacturers claimed, the world would be full of slim, happy, smart, creative people, all with a lot less disposable income. Supplements can be sold online or over the counter (i.e., without a prescription), and because they aren't regulated by the FDA, sellers are free to make whatever claims they wish. For any supplements, be sure to check with your child's doctor or at least a pharmacist. Even though they're called "supplements," some don't truly supplement but rather interfere with other drugs.

That said, researchers have found that the following three supplements have varying degrees of promise in treating mild depression in adults, although they haven't been well-studied in adolescents. They are St. John's wort (*Hypericum perforatum*), *SAMe* (*S*-adenosyl-L-methionine), and *omega-3* polyunsaturated fatty acids.

St. John's wort has been used for centuries to treat psychiatric disorders and nerve pain, and it is sold in Europe by prescription for depression. In the United States, it's available over the counter, and it is one of the top-selling herbal products. Several studies suggest it can help alleviate mild depression. But the herb has not been studied significantly in adolescents, and some studies on youth show no benefits. The most common side-effects of St. John's wort include dry mouth, dizziness, diarrhea, nausea, fatigue, and increased sensitivity to sunlight. In addition, the herbal supplement may interact with medications, including SSRIs and oral contraceptives, decreasing their effectiveness.

Several studies have found that SAMe—a synthetic version of a substance found naturally in the body—can treat symptoms of mild depression in adults. SAMe plays an important role in regulating serotonin and dopamine. Common side-effects include nausea and constipation. Don't take SAMe if you're taking prescription SSRIs, as there's a risk of serotonin syndrome. Taking SAMe may also trigger mania if your child has bipolar disorder.

Omega-3s are found in foods, including cold-water fish, such as salmon and tuna, flaxseed, walnuts, and pecans. They have anti-inflammatory properties, which may help explain why there's some evidence they may help with depression.

Be sure to talk to your child's doctor if you're thinking about trying a supplement. Just because you can buy them over the counter doesn't mean they're safe. Beware in particular of megavitamin dosing, since not only is there no evidence that it works but giving children large doses of vitamins can be fatal.

What About Just Sitting There?

Can you argue with 35 million fellow Americans? That's how many have tried meditation, according to the Centers for Disease Control and Prevention (CDC), and the numbers are growing all the time. If you stop reading right now and breathe calmly, accepting thoughts as they come and go, for just five minutes, you may get a sense of why meditation— or "mindfulness"—has become so popular in our turbulent times and why some therapists consider it a valid treatment for depression and anxiety. Although mindfulness has deep roots in Buddhist spirituality, nondenominational meditation can help almost anyone calm down, especially family members in homes in which someone is depressed. The trick—and it's a big one—is that it's much too easy to feel like there isn't time, especially when you're coping with a family crisis. Try starting for just those five minutes. Ideally, meditate together.

> "When my son was in middle school, I took him to a middle-schoolers' meditation class at a Buddhist retreat center near our home," says Beth, whose son has been diagnosed with ADHD and depression. "The teachers would have the kids run around the room to get their ya-yas out before settling down to meditate for just 15 minutes. For the rest of that evening, my son would be amazingly at peace and organized in his mind. It was one of the best things we ever tried."

From light therapy to meditation, many "alternative" methods may help a little, especially if you believe in them strongly enough. But the guiding rule should be *caveat emptor*—buyer beware. You have only so much time and money. If your child is truly suffering a serious illness, make sure to start with the best-studied conventional treatments. In Chapter 4 we'll help you figure out how to get them.

Chapter Four

Finding a Provider

N ow that you know what kinds of treatments are available, how can you find the best clinician to deliver them? Even many parents with abundant financial resources and know-how have been frustrated in trying to track down—and afford—competent mental health care for their children.

> "We needed help from someone. But when we tried to find it, it wasn't there," writes the journalist Paul Raeburn. "We took the children to a series of psychiatrists who repeatedly misdiagnosed them and treated them incorrectly, sometimes making them worse. We talked to therapists who threw us off course again and again with faulty assessments. We took the children to hospitals that did not keep them long enough to help them, because our insurance company wouldn't pay for the care. . . . We spent tens of thousands of dollars, some of the money wasted on inappropriate care, to try to fill the vast gaps in our insurance plan."

Here's the unfortunate truth, as of this writing: Even though one in five Americans has a mental health problem in any given year, mental health care is shockingly underutilized. The problems include lack of awareness about affordable treatments, insufficient coverage by insurance firms, and unavailability of suitable providers.

You're going to have to navigate a daunting, complex system. So even if you're in a genuine crisis, try giving yourself a calm window of time to move ahead. You'll need to use whatever research skills and social networks you possess to find the best, most affordable care. Along the way, you'll also need to learn about insurance plans and mental health benefits.

Why This Is Harder Than Ever

As you may already know, throughout the United States there's a serious scarcity of mental health experts—particularly psychiatrists—trained and qualified to treat adolescents. For several reasons, psychiatry has struggled to attract clinicians trained to work with youth. The specialty traditionally has required up to five years of training after medical school, which many students simply can't afford. Compounding the problem is that insurance firms are stingier with reimbursements for psychiatrists and psychotherapists than for other specialties.

At last count, there were only 9.75 US child psychiatrists for every 100,000 children under age 19. The American Academy of Child and Adolescent Psychiatry (AACAP) says we need more than four times that many. Specialists are often swamped by the demand, and the average person seeking help for a mental illness waits several weeks for a first appointment.

Many overwhelmed psychiatrists and psychologists have closed their practices to new patients, have stopped accepting payments through insurance, or are no longer able to deliver high-quality care.

> "Our psychiatrist at our HMO disappeared for seven days after Ellen was hospitalized," says Charlene. "He apologized afterward but said he had like 1,000 kids to manage. I'm sure the situation was exacerbated by the pandemic."

You may have a particularly hard search if you live far from a big city, where psychiatrists and psychologists tend to congregate. More than two-thirds of US counties lack even a single adolescent psychiatrist, meaning at best, parents will face long drives and long waits to get their children care.

Add to this another harsh reality. Many families simply can't afford psychiatric services, lack the time to ferry their kids to appointments, or are frustrated by the complexities of our mental health system. The sad result of these obstacles is that the average delay between the onset of symptoms and treatments for someone with a mental health problem in the United States is *11 years*. And only two out of ten children with mental, emotional, or behavioral disorders *ever* receive care from a specialized mental health care provider. This is especially worrying news, particularly given that mental illnesses may worsen without treatment.

Unequal Care

We have lots of advice to help you beat these odds. But first, here's one more word of warning. The hardships we've described disproportionately affect people of color and families with low incomes, not only because it's often harder for them to find and afford the care, but due to lingering stigma both within their own communities and within the medical system. African Americans, for example, are on average less likely to seek treatment for psychological symptoms. If they do, their medical providers may not be culturally competent, failing to recognize varying mood symptoms in racial groups other than their own. Researchers have found several common biases among clinicians, including that racial minorities are more immune to mental or physical pain, due to the challenges they're accustomed to facing on a regular basis. The resulting mutual distrust can complicate all kinds of medical care.

> "I can't tell you how many times I've had my children racially profiled," says Wanda, whose two daughters have been diagnosed with severe depression. "My older daughter was in a car accident, but when she got to the hospital, the nurses wouldn't give her pain medication. They assume we're addicts."

These problems help explain why people of color are more likely to be inadequately treated or remain untreated, ending up more debilitated by chronic mental illness. The unfortunate truth, if you belong to a racial minority, is that you're probably going to have to work even harder to find your child good care. The work may include overcoming both your own biases and those of your community.

> Maria and Joaquin chose not to tell relatives that they were trying medication for their depressed daughter. "We're educated and open-minded," Maria explains. "But we didn't want our daughter to have to deal with relatives who

would act as if she were broken, or we were bad parents, or she was just lazy—*floja*—and we were somehow giving in to the 'American way' and ignoring our own culture."

That's all the bad news for now. We've come to our promised suggestions for finding care for your child:

1. Rule Out Other Explanations

Before you seek care for depression, make sure that's what your child needs. Many physical problems can cause mental distress, and you'll save time, energy, and money by ruling them out before proceeding.

> The mother of a New Jersey teen who had abruptly become irritable and angry worried that he might be depressed. "The psychiatrist ordered a sleep study and found out that he had sleep apnea, which was causing the symptoms," she said.

Ask your child's regular doctor for a thorough physical evaluation. Potentially confusing conditions can include head injury, hypothyroidism, anemia, mononucleosis, Lyme disease, chronic fatigue syndrome, hepatitis, side-effects of medication, and substance use disorders or withdrawal.

2. Aim for the Gold Standard

Once you've established that your child is indeed battling depression, your ideal clinician would be a board-certified adolescent psychiatrist to prescribe and monitor medication, *and* a psychotherapist to provide talk therapy. Some psychiatrists can fulfill both these roles.

In the rare situation that you have a choice of specialists, compare their training and experience in adolescent mood disorders, as well as fees and payment policies, the type of insurance accepted, if any, and office hours and location. If you can't find a psychiatrist who specializes in adolescents, be open to seeing one who treats adults. All psychiatrists must at least have some training with minors.

Maria's online search for care for her depressed daughter brought her to the Columbia University Clinic for Anxiety & Related Disorders in Manhattan, one of many US centers combining research and clinical care. There was a $25 co-pay per visit, and her insurance plan paid 80% only after she reached her $3,000 annual family deductible. "It was quite expensive," she says. But she was thrilled with the cutting-edge care that her daughter received.

In a pinch, pediatricians and nurse practitioners may be willing to prescribe medication for depression. But don't have them do that if the illness is complicated or severe, since they likely will lack the right training and experience.

3. Enlist Your Child's Pediatrician in Your Search

Pediatricians can often help you find the right specialist. They know the local professional landscape as well as anyone and are likely invested in helping your child.

"Our son's pediatrician is so helpful and aware of our family's needs!" Stephanie wrote in an email. "When Gary became depressed, she discovered it first. We'd thought he was just sad that his dog died. She gave us several contacts for psychiatrists and counselors and helped us find him the right medication."

Some pediatricians categorically refuse to prescribe medications for mental illness. Yet once your child is established on a medication, many will agree to step in to monitor and continue the prescriptions, ideally in consultation with a psychiatrist. One more suggestion: If your daughter's mood is plunging on schedule each month, consider asking her doctor for birth-control pills that can combat premenstrual blues.

4. Check Out These National Referral Services

These organizations and others we list in the Resources section can help with your search for affordable mental health care:

The National Alliance on Mental Illness (NAMI) has a
    helpline for free assistance Monday through Friday, 10
    a.m. to 10 p.m. EST. You can reach the helpline at 1-800-
    950-6264. NAMI also offers a free, 24/7 crisis text: just
    text 988.
The Substance Abuse and Mental Health Services
    Administration (SAMHSA), a government agency, pro-
    vides a treatment locator for low-cost facilities.
The National Association of Free & Charitable Clinics,
    Mental Health America, and the Open Path Psychotherapy
    Collective also provide online tools to find affordable men-
    tal health services.

5. Be a Smart Health Care Consumer

If you're like most modern parents, you'll start your search for help on the internet. Maybe you'll also try to educate yourself about depression online. On balance, the internet has been a boon for consumers seeking to educate themselves and compare products and services. But beware: It's also a haven for hucksters who prey on the panicked and vulnerable. Aim for information from websites ending in .edu, for "educational." The .com suffix means "commercial," and you'll see it on sites offering services for pay. Don't believe everything you read on .com sites, and make sure that any provider you engage has genuine credentials and isn't trying to sell a fringe therapy.

Check out potential providers online on your state's medical board website, where you can confirm they have a license and see if they've had any complaints against them. You may also want to look at review sites, like Yelp, Healthgrades, RateMDs.com, and Vitals.com, but don't take them at their word. Satisfied clients of psychiatrists and therapists rarely want to violate their own privacy, but cranks tend not to worry about that, so these reviews may be misrepresentative and misleading.

6. Trust Your Gut

If you don't think your child's doctor is seeing what you're seeing, keep asking questions—or change doctors.

"My parents stopped at nothing to help me along the way," says Lisa Himmel, 20 years after her crises with depression and anorexia. "They dove into research and fully supported any form or method of treatment I either sought out or was recommended. What worked best for us was being open to trying, whether that was trying new therapists or new programs or medication. We just had to keep trying."

7. When Choosing Psychotherapists, Keep an Eye on the Relationship

As we've mentioned, your child will likely need a therapist to talk to, perhaps in addition to medication. Beyond making sure that the professional is licensed and has a good reputation, you don't need to worry too much if the therapy is called "psychodynamic" or cognitive-behavioral or interpersonal, as long as your child willingly shows up for appointments and seems to trust the process. The "therapeutic bond" is essential for progress.

> "When Lisa was hospitalized, a friend recommended a psychologist who not only understood eating disorders, but bonded with Lisa," says Lisa's mother, the author and journalist Sheila Himmel. "Lisa quickly came to trust her and gradually got her life back. Of course this therapist was out-of-network for our insurance and expensive. But she made Lisa feel heard and understood."

Be aware if your child isn't bonding with the therapist, since that would doom the process. You may have a few false starts before you find someone truly effective.

Care in a Crisis

Increasingly, parents of children suffering from acute mood disorders who engage in self-harm and suicidal behavior have resorted to hospital emergency rooms. For more information on hospitalization in a crisis and other emergency services, including controversial "wilderness programs," turn to Chapter 9.

Professional Help: Who Does What?

Several different kinds of professionals provide mental health services. We rank these below according to years of training, noting who can prescribe medication or provide psychotherapy.

Type of Professional	May Prescribe Medication?	May Provide Psychotherapy?
Psychiatrists	Yes	Yes
Primary care physicians	Yes	No
Psychiatric nurses	Yes, with advanced training	Yes
Clinical psychologists	No*	Yes
Clinical social workers	No	Yes
Mental health counselors	No	Yes
Marriage and family therapists	No	Yes

* Psychologists aren't trained as physicians, which limits them when it comes to prescribing and monitoring medication. Yet they can legally prescribe medications in five states: Louisiana, New Mexico, Illinois, Iowa, and Idaho. They may also prescribe medications anywhere in the US military and the Indian Health Service if they are credentialed in Louisiana or New Mexico.

When Should You Enlist a Developmental Behavioral Pediatrician?

Developmental behavioral pediatricians (also known as developmental-behavioral pediatricians) are trained and certified to evaluate and treat children and adolescents with a wide range of neurodevelopmental or behavioral disorders that may coexist with mood disorders such as depression. These include attention-deficit/hyperactivity disorder (ADHD), tics, learning disorders such as dyslexia, and developmental disabilities such as cerebral palsy, spina bifida, and autism spectrum disorder. These specialists usually practice in hospitals, clinics, and rehabilitation centers, although some can be found in private practice. They're usually in short supply outside big cities.

What About a Neuropsychologist?

Your child's primary doctor or mental health professional may suggest an appointment with a neuropsychologist. In most cases, this is to see if there's a problem with cognition—thinking—concentration, or memory, which may affect learning. The doctor may suspect that a brain injury, illness, or developmental problem is contributing to the depression. A neuropsychologist may be particularly helpful if you're seeking accommodations at your child's school and need to establish a diagnosis of a specific disorder, as we'll further explain later. Yet a thorough evaluation, which could include several cognitive tests, can be expensive. In rare cases, public schools will pay, although it may require a lawyer's intervention. The advantage is that you'll learn a great deal about the way your child's brain works, from processing speed to memory to impulsivity. This can help you clarify the diagnosis and figure out what to do next.

How Do You Build Rapport With Your Provider?

You can contribute to your child's important bond with the provider in several ways. Let it be known that you have faith in the process and are available to answer any questions. Pay your bills on time and respect the provider's limited time, knowing he or she is probably swamped all day with appointments, calls, and emails. Make contact only when truly needed; use cellphone numbers, if offered, only in emergencies, and if you have time-consuming concerns, consider scheduling a paid appointment to discuss them. Most therapists will schedule a separate session for a parent to help with common dilemmas such as whether it's advisable to let a kid stay home from school occasionally for a mental health day.

Make a point of telling your doctor about your child's strengths as well as the problems. Try not to be defensive but also don't be afraid to switch if the relationship isn't working out.

How Should You Prepare for Appointments?

When meeting for the first time with your child's mental health care provider, come prepared to answer questions about behaviors that concern you. You may be asked when they started, how often they occur, how long they last, and how severe they seem. Don't neglect to fill out questionnaires that many clinicians now provide before a first appointment, so that they can spend more time talking with you and your child. The provider may also wish to communicate by phone or email with teachers, social services workers, and the primary care doctor. He or she will want to know if there have been any major new stresses or changes in the patient's life, and if any first- or second-degree blood relatives (the latter including aunts and uncles, grandparents, and nephews and nieces) have suffered from mood disorders.

Before the appointment, it will help for you to write down some of the answers to these questions. Make sure to also make a list of all medications, vitamins, herbs, or other supplements being taken, and in what doses.

You're likely to be nervous during the appointment, so it will save time and avoid errors to do all of this record-keeping in advance. You may want to make a written timeline to illustrate when your child's problems first appeared, including any events that may have triggered them.

Digital Care and Telepsychiatry

The COVID-19 pandemic gave a big boost to a trend, already underway, toward internet options for health care, including psychotherapy. Seemingly overnight, mental health providers got used to scheduling meetings with patients on platforms such as Zoom.

The pandemic also fueled rapid growth in services allowing patients to text with their therapists. Online counseling services such as Talkspace, which is covered by many major insurers, and BetterHelp are much cheaper than traditional in-person therapy. Still, the results of this trend have been mixed. On one hand, the advent of "telehealth" has helped address the shortage of all kinds of providers by eliminating the need for patients to commute and giving them a much broader geographical choice. And some adolescents, especially at first, may feel less wary of meeting with a therapist online.

Still, many mental health providers worry that the move to two-dimensional settings, and in particular to therapy by text, diminishes those crucial therapeutic relationships that would otherwise benefit from all the subtle nonverbal communication that goes on within the walls of an office. As a practical matter, therapists don't get a full view of their patients online, meaning they may easily miss visual clues to self-harm or abuse. What's more, many low-income families are up against a "digital divide," lacking adequate systems of WiFi and computers or even a quiet, private room for therapy sessions.

Despite these limitations, however, this trend isn't going away—just the opposite. Figure out what suits you best. The best option may be a hybrid model, allowing your child to participate in person for the most important meetings. For psychotherapy, however, we recommend you opt for the in-person, personal relationship if possible.

What Other Mental Health Services Are Available?

A variety of options for treatment fall along the continuum between occasional visits to a therapist or physician and crisis response, such as emergency hospitalization. The following are for those with at least some time to choose:

- *Residential treatment centers*—These facilities provide round-the-clock supervision and care in a locked, dorm-like setting. The treatment is less specialized and intensive

than in a hospital, but the length of stay is often considerably longer. We will tell you more about them in
Chapter 9.

• *Partial hospitalization or day treatment*—Outpatient services such as individual and group therapy, vocational
training, parent counseling, and therapeutic recreational activities are provided for at least four hours per
day. The adolescent receives intensive services during
the day but may go home at night. Some websites refer
to these programs by their initials—IOP for intensive
outpatient program, or PHP for partial hospitalization
program. The difference is mainly in the number of
hours. An IOP might be three hours three times a week,
often after school, for instance, while a PHP would
be a full-time program, say from 9 a.m. to 3 p.m. If
your child has a combination of problems, you may
want to seek a "dual diagnosis program," which might,
for example, simultaneously treat depression and substance use disorder.

• *Home-based services*—Treatment is provided in the adolescent's home; for example, help with implementing
a behavior therapy plan, medication management, or
training for parents and adolescents on how to keep
the illness from becoming a crisis. Providers include
some state-funded programs and university health systems. The goal is to improve family coping skills and
avert the need for more expensive services, such as
hospitalization.

• *Respite care*—You may be able to receive child care provided by trained parents or mental health aides for a
short period of time. This provides families with a much-
needed breather from the strain of caring for an ill child,

which may include a child with a serious mood disorder. Sounds great, right? Alas, respite care is hard to come by. Some families report finding this support through Medicaid, but the policy varies from state to state and usually comes with strict limits.

- *Mentoring programs*—For several years, a program called Vive, headquartered in Boulder, Colorado, offered a hybrid therapeutic program which would assign a trained mentor to a struggling child and a therapist to coach the parents. The organization has since changed its mission, but the idea was inspired, so if you hear of any copycats, it's worth a try. Simply finding a young adult, perhaps an energetic college student, to spend time with your child can be a great form of respite care! Look for mentoring programs designed for at-risk kids and offered by your local community center.

Once again, your child's doctor or your managed care program may be the best source of information about these sorts of services. If those sources fail, try seeking accredited programs on the internet—you might google the name of your county and a phrase like "teen mental health." (In this case, don't be deterred by those .com suffixes, because you are looking for services to buy.) You can also ask other parents, your child's school counselor, a clergyperson, social service agencies, or the mental health division of your local health department.

What Is a "System of Care"?

For adolescents with severe mental illness, it's especially helpful to combine standard treatment with other types of support.

This is known as a "system of care"—a collaborative network of mental health and social services. Since mental illness touches every facet of a young person's life, the best treatment may indeed require many kinds of services from a variety of sources, including the child's school.

Ideally, you'll be able to coordinate a team working in and out of school to plan and implement services tailored to your adolescent's emotional, physical, educational, and social needs. Depending on the situation, team members might include the family doctor, a psychiatrist, a school psychologist, vocational counseling, substance-misuse counseling, perhaps a sports coach, and if you're truly unfortunate, a probation officer. But the key word here is "ideally."

In reality, such teamwork is the happy exception rather than the rule. More likely you'll be enlisting helpers one by one.

What Is Collaborative Care?

A growing use of collaborative, or "integrated," practices throughout the United States aims to compensate for the shortage of child and adolescent psychiatrists and to ensure that adolescents receive care as early as possible. This model helps psychiatrists leverage their time by consulting with others with less specialized experience. (In some cases, psychotherapists will work in the same offices as primary care doctors.) The psychiatrists, who may have offices far from the patients' homes, work mainly as consultants to specially trained nurse practitioners, seeing patients directly only when absolutely needed.

Mental Health Care Isn't Cheap

- Approximate cost of a single outpatient therapy session, in most parts of the United States: $100–$200
- Average cost of inpatient care for youths who need psychiatric hospitalization: $6,990 for 8.4 days for depression
- Approximate cost of 1 year at a wilderness program: $513/day, with an average cost of $250,000
- Percentage of US health plans in 2013 that included coverage for mental health treatment: 61

What Should You Know About Health Insurance?

For many parents, one of the greatest challenges in helping a struggling child will be figuring out how to pay for care. Millions of Americans lack any insurance coverage, much less for mental health services. Many of those who do have coverage often find that it is inadequate.

"Our deductible is way too high, but I didn't realize that until we had to pay it," says Jeanne.

Most Americans who have insurance at this writing receive it through a managed care plan, such as those run by Kaiser Permanente, the largest US operation, or Blue Cross or Anthem. We'll describe how this works in more detail below, but the key point is that most of these firms seek to lower costs by having patients get care from doctors with whom they contract to belong to their "networks." Most also impose some restrictions on mental health benefits, such as limiting the number of outpatient sessions or inpatient days that are covered. In addition, private insurance rarely if ever covers the full spectrum of community- and home-based services that adolescents with severe depression may need to continue living with their families.

"We spent a total of about $200,000 on therapists, psychiatrists, in-patient treatment, and a wilderness camp," says Charlene. "We took the money from our retirement funds, which means my husband and I will have to keep working, like, forever. But I know we're still luckier than lots of other parents. I don't know how most people afford this."

Even with all these problems, the situation has improved a lot since 2010, after the enactment of the Affordable Care Act (aka the ACA, or "Obamacare"). The ACA made health insurance available to more than 18 million Americans who didn't previously have it. It expanded many states' Medicaid budgets—although some states refused to take the money— and provided families with incomes below 400% of the federal poverty level with tax credits to reduce their health costs. It has also required insurance plans to cover people with preexisting health conditions and allowed young adults to stay on their parents' plans until age 26.

If you don't already have insurance, or aren't covered through Medicare, Medicaid, or the Children's Health Insurance Program (CHIP), which we'll describe in more detail below, you can sign up for a plan during a period of time once a year—usually starting in November—at www.healthcare.gov. There, you may choose among a "marketplace" of health insurance options, which will vary according to your state's policies. What you pay for insurance through the marketplace will depend on your income. You can reach on-call, free advisors with questions about health insurance at https://www.healt hsherpa.com/

What Is Parity?

A major goal of the ACA is to ensure "parity" for mental health services. Health advocates and lawmakers have sought this for many years. Parity means that mental health and substance-abuse benefits can't be more restrictive than for other medical conditions. In other words, deductibles, co-payments, and out-of-pocket limits for mental health care *should* be equal to those pertaining to other types of care. This provision, plus prior guarantees in the 2008 Mental Health Parity and Addiction Equity Act, has indeed led to many more people getting mental health care at reduced costs. But they certainly haven't solved the problem.

Researchers have found that disparities between physical and mental health care have continued in recent years and even widened in some cases, in part due to noncompliance by some insurance plans. Many firms are simply violating the new laws, and many patients don't know how to defend themselves. (See below.) Another glaring issue is that with so many mental health professionals not accepting insurance, patients are often more likely to have to go outside their managed care network and pay more.

Fight Back

Here are some signs that your health insurance plan may be trying to cut costs at the expense of your family's mental health:

- *"Fail-first" policies.* A health plan may use a "fail-first" policy, denying mental health treatment, such as hospital care, because the health plan member hasn't tried and failed at a lower level of care (e.g., outpatient care). This may be illegal if the plan doesn't have a similar policy for medical care.
- *Limits on the quantity or frequency of outpatient treatment.* Some health plans cap the number of outpatient mental

health visits allowed each year, without similarly limiting outpatient medical visits. The plan may also limit mental health visits to once a week or every other week without similar provisions for medical visits.

- *More restrictive prior authorization policies* for behavioral health. Many health plans require prior authorization for nonemergency inpatient hospital services, both medical and mental health. Yet they may have different lengths of time allowed, for instance just one day for mental health versus a week for medical care.

(Excerpted from a handout prepared by Health Law Advocates, a national nonprofit organization)

You can read the full handout, including advice for how to help enforce the laws, in the Resources section. Patients who suspect violations should contact their state's insurance commissioner's office. If the plan is through a large employer, you can submit a complaint directly to the federal Employee Benefit Security Administration (EBSA), reachable online at www.askebsa.dol.gov. If the plan is a Medicaid Managed Care plan, your state Office of Medicaid is responsible for enforcing the parity laws.

Remember, you have the right to appeal any denied claim. Ask your doctor for support with this if necessary.

Watch Out for "Carve-outs"!

Make sure when you choose a health insurance plan to ask about mental health "carve-outs." This is a sneaky way that some insurance companies have used to try to cut expenses. You may assume, for instance, that if you sign up for Blue Shield, you will have access to Blue Shield mental health services, only to find out, after you submit your first claim, that you don't! As of 2012, Blue Shield carved out mental health services to another company, Magellan, which paid less to providers. As a consumer, you will need to ask lots of questions each time you pick a mental health provider to make sure they are covered by your network.

Health insurance is complicated. You can find out more information and ask questions of on-call advisers on a federal government site, https://www.healthsherpa.com/. But keep three rules in mind. Don't risk going without insurance, because you may be in for some lavish expenses. Second: Be aware that you can now keep your child covered through early adulthood. Third: If you have a choice, compare available plans, looking closely at coverage for mental health services.

How Should You Choose a Managed Care Plan?

Managed care was designed to control health care costs, through a system in which insurers sign contracts with groups of providers who agree in advance to certain prices for diverse procedures. You can compare your options for a plan by typing your zip code on the HealthSherpa site noted above. (You can also call: 872-228-2549.) The tool will also let you know if you are eligible for subsidies. Some states offer Medicaid Managed Care plans.

There are several different types of plans, including the following:

- *Health maintenance organizations* (HMOs)—requiring you to sign up with a primary care doctor and use other health care providers who work for the HMO's network.

You will usually need a referral from your primary doctor for mental health services.

- *Preferred provider organizations* (PPOs)—allowing you to choose from a network of providers who have contracts with the PPO but also providing some benefits if you choose an outside provider. With this plan, you're less likely to need a referral from your primary care doctor to get access to a mental health care provider. If you go outside the network, you'll have to pay more. This plan also has higher monthly premiums.

- *Exclusive provider organizations* (EPOs)—requiring you to receive all your nonemergency services (if you want them covered) with doctors, specialists, or hospitals in the plan's network. This is the most restrictive but least expensive plan, with the least coverage of out-of-network providers.

- *Point of service (POS) plans*—allowing a choice of providers outside the HMO organization or PPO network. Higher co-payments and deductibles are the downside.

If you can choose among several managed care plans, be sure to compare the benefit packages. Check for clauses that restrict covered services, such as caps on the number of outpatient visits allowed per year or exclusions of certain medications from the approved drug list. If you already have a favorite doctor or therapist, investigate whether that person is in the provider network. Otherwise, look for a comprehensive network, including some providers located near your home. Finally, consider the co-payments and deductibles you'll have to pay. And try to get a feel for the administrative hassles you'll face once you try to access care. Note: You can cancel and change your managed care plan at any time.

Ghosted

Many a beleaguered parent has been haunted by "ghost networks." That's when an insurance company offers you a list of supposedly living and breathing psychiatrists who either don't answer your calls or are no longer taking new patients or have stopped taking insurance. But have no fear! If this is the case, and you've made a reasonable effort to try their list, you can often apply for a "single-case agreement," in which your insurance plan covers an out-of-network provider for the same cost to you as if it were in-network. If your child is a new patient, you can request a single-case agreement if you can't find an in-network provider near your home, if the treatment provided will reduce the cost of medications or keep your child out of the hospital, or if your child needs a certain type of therapy not offered by the network providers. Just make sure you apply for this before starting treatment. One more tip: If you find the claim process overwhelming, there's help online. Check out sites like Reimbursify, which can help with the process, sometimes for a fee.

Key Takeaways for Managed Care

- Familiarize yourself with the plan's provisions—in particular, the cost of premiums, deductibles, and co-pays.
- Get to know your primary care provider as soon as possible.
- Work out a plan for services for your child.
- Figure out in advance whom to call and where to go in an emergency.
- Get any required preauthorization for nonemergency services.

- Learn about the procedure for appealing a treatment denial.
- Be sure to provide positive feedback when things go smoothly.

How Can You Influence Managed Care Decisions?

One of the main cost-cutting tools used by managed care plans is the "utilization review," a formal review of health care services to determine whether payment for them should be authorized or denied. In making this determination, the managed care company considers two factors: whether the services are covered under your health insurance plan and whether the services meet the standard for "medical necessity." Most treatment denials are based on the medical necessity provision. This is a situation in which your health insurance plan covers the services a doctor or therapist recommends, but the managed care company decides not to pay for them because they aren't deemed medically necessary.

Sue's health plan initially authorized an emergency hospitalization for her son at the closest available facility, even though it wasn't in the plan's care network. The next morning, however, "they wanted us to move him, despite his fragile state. He was catatonic. I fought with the insurance company, and I was finally told he could stay." A few weeks later, though, Sue was surprised to receive a large bill. Despite what the representative had told her on the phone, the health plan had denied coverage for part of her son's hospitalization, claiming it wasn't medically necessary for him to remain in that facility.

Managed care companies are required to inform customers of how to appeal a denial of services. If you do so, enlist the help of the health care provider who recommended the treatment. If you're seeking preapproval for emergency services, an expedited appeals process should be available. But if it's after the fact or the situation isn't an emergency, getting a decision may take time. It took Sue more than three months to appeal her health plan's decision, but she ultimately won coverage of her son's hospital stay.

If your first appeal is denied, ask your plan to provide written notification of the reasons and to tell you what information is needed for the treatment to be approved. You can always appeal again. Most managed care companies have three or four levels of appeal, each involving a different set of people.

Help is available if you encounter problems at any point in the appeals process. For employer-provided insurance, your company's human resources department may be able to help. For Medicaid issues, your state may have an ombudsman, whose job it is to try to resolve consumer complaints. Local mental health organizations may also be able to provide helpful advice. If you exhaust your appeals without success, the managed care company and your provider should agree on an acceptable alternative to the treatment originally requested.

Although it may seem daunting, many parents learn to become effective in battling bureaucracies on behalf of their children.

> "At one point, I had something like 60 days of hospitalization available to my daughter and only $500 in therapy," says Julie. "I called the insurance company and convinced them to give us more therapy dollars as a trade-off for some of the hospitalization days."

What Financial Help Is Available?

Many parents haven't been told that public schools will sometimes foot the bill for some services for children in need. They do this as part of an individualized education program (IEP), something we'll explain in depth in Chapter 7. Typically the services are limited to diagnosis and evaluation, but sometimes go beyond that to include counseling and other interventions. This could be one of those cases where if you don't ask, you don't get, so make sure to ask. You may be surprised.

Many clinicians, when paid out of pocket, may cut you some slack. Ask if they have sliding scales.

Federally qualified health centers are community-based providers that receive federal funds to provide care to underserved groups, such as migrants, homeless, and public-housing residents. They aren't allowed to turn anyone away, and you don't have to have insurance. You can find these clinics in your area by looking online.

Medicaid, paid for by a combination of federal and state funds, is by far the biggest US payer for community- and home-based health services of all kinds. Medicaid provides care to more than 72 million Americans who live in poverty. It is supplemented by CHIP, which delivers coverage for children whose families have a slightly higher income level. CHIP will pay for routine checkups, immunizations, doctor visits, prescriptions, dental and vision care, emergency services, X-rays, and more. Each state has its own rules about who qualifies, but in most states, children in a family of four earning up to $50,000 a year will be eligible. If you apply for Medicaid coverage in your state, you'll find out if your children qualify for CHIP. You can apply for and enroll in Medicaid and CHIP at any time of the year. Most of the care is free, but there may be some co-payments or monthly premiums for coverage. This also varies in each state, but by law can't be more than 5% of your family's income.

If you have private insurance and your child has a chronic condition, you may be able to have Medicaid as a secondary insurance—potentially a huge advantage. In this case, your primary policy will pick up normal costs while the Medicaid plan covers co-pays, and sometimes also the deductible, minimizing your out-of-pocket costs.

Some Medicaid recipients say the system has shielded them from the scarcity of private adolescent psychiatrists.

"I've found it a lot easier to glean services through public assistance as the doctors are already in place at public family service organizations," says Mary, a mother and graduate student in San Jose. "It's true they're not always top notch. We had problems with two who prescribed drugs that were totally wrong for my son. But I have to admit I feel a little better about it all after hearing all the stories of how other parents struggle with trying to find a psychiatrist within their private health plans."

Unfortunately, many middle-class families aren't eligible for Medicaid and CHIP. These families find themselves in a classic double bind: They don't make enough money to pay for costly mental health services out of pocket, but they make too much to qualify for government programs.

The "Katie Beckett" option offers one small ray of hope for these parents. The law, adopted by 18 states and the District of Columbia, is part of the Tax Equity and Fiscal Responsibility Act of 1982 (TEFRA) and is named after a woman in Iowa who as a child had suffered major respiratory issues. (Beckett died in 2012, at the age of 34.) It requires the adopting states to pay for extensive care for children under the age of 19 who have complex medical needs or long-term disabilities, and who are living at home and might otherwise have to be institutionalized. Eligibility is based on the child's income and assets, with no regard for the parents' status, and states cannot limit the number of participants. The downside is that the laws are confusing and vary according to state, so if this is of interest it might be worth consulting with an attorney.

Other encouraging news comes from Colorado, where state legislators recently decided to improve adolescent mental health care after a slew of school shootings by students struggling with their mental health. Colorado had ranked 48th among US states in terms of high prevalence of mental illness but low access to care in a major national report. But in 2018, a new law doubled the state's youth mental health budget. Proponents of the law said it would help families stay together, with children receiving services at home instead of institutions.

> "It's called the Colorado Youth Mental Health Treatment Act, and I thank heaven for it," says the mother of a suicidal teen in the Denver area who was able to have a family therapist come to their home in the wake of a crisis. "It pays for more services that my insurance ever would have done."

If you've got a job, be sure to look into whether your company offers discounted or free mental health benefits via an employee assistance program. Also take advantage, if you need to, of any family leave your workplace offers for family medical issues. The federal Family and Medical Leave Act guarantees that eligible employees are covered for up to 12 weeks of unpaid leave in a 12-month period (during which the employer must keep the job open) for several reasons, including to care for a spouse, child, or parent with a serious health condition. Those who've accumulated a bank of sick leave days can often use those, with no loss of income. All government workers and grade-school teachers are covered by this law, as are most private employers with at least 50 employees.

If finding treatment for your child sounds hit or miss, it is. Some savvy parents learn to work the system. But it takes time, energy, and a high tolerance for frustration. Not surprisingly, many parents say that financial concerns are among the most stressful aspects of raising an adolescent with depression. It's not just the bills. Some parents find they can't keep their jobs due to all the time they're spending, both in seeking treatment and providing care at home for their child in distress. Some even intentionally let their careers slide so that they can qualify for low-income programs. Still others with good jobs and above-average benefits nevertheless find themselves in an exhausting, never-ending struggle to make ends meet.

> As one mother, whose husband is a successful consulting engineer, says: "It doesn't matter how hard he works or how much money he makes. There's never enough. We haven't gone on a real vacation in four years. We don't have money to go out or fix up our house. Every penny goes to taking care of the kids, and it's still not enough."

Amid all the alarms about our mental illness epidemic, the federal government and many state agencies are trying to find better options. We'll tell you about some of them in the Conclusion. For now, however, you may need to keep fighting with your insurance plan and managed care system to pay for the treatments your child needs, without letting all that stress interfere with the atmosphere at home.

Chapter Five

Helping at Home

Perhaps by now you've found your son or daughter medical treatment and maybe also psychotherapy. Bravo! These are major, and, alas, rare achievements. Still, that new job you've taken on shouldn't end here. To help your child combat depression and keep it at bay, there's a lot more that you can do right at home.

You may be wondering how much difference you can make, given that some experts insist that genes and peers will always trump a parent's power. And indeed, you can't do much about the biology and twists of fate affecting your child's mental health. Yet you can still have enormous influence. You do so with the behavior you model, the warmth of your relationship, where you live—if you have a choice—and the serenity and structure you provide in your home.

Threats and Defenses

Researchers have found several potential contributors to depression and also several factors that can help reduce their influence. These are also known as "risk factors" and "protective factors." Fewer risk factors and more protective ones may reduce the severity and duration of episodes of depression. A healthy mix might even prevent depression from emerging in the first place in children at risk.

The chart below lists some of these threats and defenses. Notice which ones you can and can't influence.

Risk Factors

Genes: a family history of depression

Trauma: a death, accident, or loss

Conflict: personal turmoil with family or friends

Poverty

Harmful use of drugs or alcohol by the parents or child

Academic failure

Physical, sexual, or emotional abuse, including bullying at school

Stressful life events, including transitions such as moving or graduating from school

Other problems, including physical illnesses, sleep disturbances, anxiety, attention-deficit/hyperactivity disorder (ADHD), and/or learning differences

(Beginning in early 2020, the COVID-19 pandemic added another set of challenges. A child was more at risk of depression for several reasons, including living in an area with more severe outbreaks, having caregivers who were also front-line workers, having caregivers at higher risk of burnout [including due to increased parenting demands], having disruptions in routines, including going to school in person, and experiencing trauma, such as losing a family member or caregiver due to COVID-19.)

Protective Factors

Supportive family relationships
A sense of physical and emotional safety
Predictable home life with structure and rules
Parental warmth and strong attachment
Healthy habits, including sleep, diet, and exercise
Connections to community, including supportive adults
  outside the family
Optimism
Success at school
Development of skills

The bottom line is that medication and psychotherapy can work wonders, but they're still not enough. Your child will need a variety of environmental supports and healthy habits to ward off harmful moods. You might think of these as a toolkit that you can help assemble, with four priorities for the sorts of tools you'll need. To help keep them in mind, imagine writing a note to yourself, with the acronym PSPS. It stands for Peace, Sleep (and nutrition), Predictability, and Strength. Making progress on these four fronts is your best hope for getting your child and your family on track.

Peace

While chaos at home may not cause mood disorders in children, it will surely make them worse. Chronic stress, as we've already noted, may harm the brain, and it may contribute to depression. That's why your priority in helping a child with depression must be to keep things calm at home.

We realize this is no small task. Living with a depressed adolescent can bring out the worst in almost anyone. Families can

get trapped in a vicious cycle, in which an irritable, uncooperative child provokes conflict that aggravates the child's bad
behavior. If you've come to feel like a hostage in your own
home, you've unfortunately got plenty of company.

Appropriate treatment for the child's depression will be your
best first move to break the cycle of conflict. Sometimes other
family members or even the whole family may need therapy
as well. Yet even that may not suffice. If you are locked in
irrevocable marital conflict, or if your spouse is abusive to any
of your kids, or if a sibling is posing a clear and present danger to anyone else in the home, you're going to have to make
some tough decisions. Don't hesitate to get the help you need,
even if it means enlisting local government agencies or leaning
on relatives or friends to provide a temporary sanctuary for a
sibling. It may be embarrassing to ask for such help, but it's a
small price to pay to avoid physical or emotional injuries.

On that topic, we urge you to avoid the temptation to
physically punish your child, no matter how frustrated or
scared you may be. Maybe your own parents spanked you,
or their parents spanked them, but in the past few decades,
overwhelming evidence has shown that corporal punishment
causes more problems than it cures. Not only will physically
hurting your child fail to teach good behavior; you can all but
guarantee that the behavior will worsen over time. Many parents have found that getting therapy or coaching helps them
find alternatives.

Do's and Don'ts of Keeping the Peace
Do . . .

- Choose your battles. Avoid getting into arguments over
  issues that aren't worth the emotional strain.

- Wait until you've both cooled off to talk it over. State the problem and explain your perspective calmly.
- Be sure to ask your child to share thoughts on the matter. Give that viewpoint careful consideration.
- Use humor to defuse a tense situation, if possible. Just make sure it isn't an angry or sarcastic remark disguised as a "joke."
- Seek a compromise, if one is available. When you need to assert your authority, be calm but firm.
- Apologize when you know you were wrong.
- Use "I" statements to avoid placing all of the blame on the adolescent, since that can lead to standoffs. Rather than say: "You always come home late," try: "I noticed that you came home later that we agreed on, and I get very upset when that happens because I worry about your safety."

Don't . . .

- Let your child hijack your emotions. If you find yourself getting angry, take some deep breaths; count to 10, or excuse yourself for a couple of minutes to calm down. You might also call a friend, divide and conquer with your partner, or seek help from family and friends.
- Take things personally or expect an adolescent in the grips of depression to be receptive to reasoning. Your child is flooded with emotions that will likely prevent a rational response in that moment.
- Hold a grudge or let angry outbursts become a habit in your family. If conflict has become a frequent or severe problem, consider family therapy.

Explanation or Excuse?

If your child has become irritable and oppositional, you may find yourself asking the vexing question of how much of the behavior is a choice. Is he or she manipulating you, or is this part of the illness? No one wants to raise a spoiled child, but nor should you punish disobedience that's unintentional. It's worth asking yourself: Do you habitually lean toward empathy or toward insisting that every rule is followed? Do you easily take things personally? Kids with depression can be unintentionally forgetful, stubborn, surly, and even hurtful. But the insults that fly during a conflict may be less about you than your child's own feelings of self-loathing.

If your child is seriously depressed, this is no time to sweat the small stuff. You'll need to choose which behaviors are absolute no-go's (such as hitting a sibling) and which aren't worth an argument (such as sneaking in an extra half-hour of video games). You may occasionally also need to broaden your perspective and imagine what your child's day was like, if he or she was teased or rejected or couldn't keep track in class. Sometimes a parent's tough talk is needed, but beware of the times when it might make things worse.

> "At one point I just realized that he felt everyone else in the world was against him, and I had to be the one person who was on his side," says the mother of an adult in Utah who grew up with depression and ADHD.

The Buddhist teacher and clinical psychologist Tara Brach has coined an acronym that may be helpful for you in dealing with all the difficult emotions your child may evoke. It's called "RAIN," for:

Recognize what is happening;
Allow the experience to be there, as it is;
Investigate with interest and care;
Nurture with self-compassion.

Give yourself the calm mental space to be curious about the reasons for your child's behavior before you react.

Sleep and Diet

A key prerequisite for preserving domestic peace is to help your child get sufficient sleep. Several large studies have found clear connections between sleep disturbances and mental health. What's more, sleep deprivation can contribute to physical problems, including obesity, diabetes, heart disease, the self-destructive use of drugs and alcohol, and vehicle crashes. The connection is so clear that researchers in the ABCD study, the largest, long-term US evaluation of child brain development, called sleep "a tool to mitigate the persistence of depression across early adolescence." Good sleep habits, they surmised, might even prevent the onset of depression.

Sleep is paramount for anyone's physical and mental health yet is often undermined by mental illness. Depressed kids may have trouble falling asleep, leaving them exhausted the next day. Meanwhile, your child's problems with sleep may be ruining *your* sleep, especially as late-night emotional crises find their way past your bedroom door.

"Even as a toddler, Ellen used to wake up with night terrors," says Charlene. "Then once she was a teen, I used to wake up in the night and see her switch off her light if she heard me coming. It got so that either I was already up at night worrying about her or she would wake me by prowling through the house, which was always a warning that things weren't well."

Helping a child with depression sleep soundly through the night is easier said than done. Many parents never master it. Complicating everything are biological changes that begin in puberty, when kids start falling asleep about two hours later and then naturally wanting to sleep later in the morning. This sets them—and you—up for a major predicament.

The American Academy of Sleep Medicine recommends that children ages 6 to 12 should sleep from 9 to 12 hours per day and that teenagers 13 to 18 sleep 8 to 10 hours. Yet a 2013 Centers for Disease Control and Prevention (CDC) study found that 68% of US high school students reported getting less than 8 hours of sleep on school nights. Your kid isn't just being stubborn. Part of the issue is that most adolescents' sleep patterns aren't in sync with their school schedules.

Both the American Academy of Pediatrics and the CDC recommend that middle and high schools start no earlier than 8:30 a.m. Unfortunately, at last count, more than 90% of US high schools and 83% of middle schools were ignoring that guidance.

Schools' unsupportive schedules lead to ongoing arguments between parents and kids—especially kids whose depression already makes them irritable. You may find yourself cajoling your wide-awake child to go to bed early and then, the next morning, urging your drowsy child to get out of bed for school.

If your child has a diagnosed mood disorder, you may be able to arrange a later schedule at school as part of the accommodations we'll explain in Chapter 7. Short of that, we suggest you help your child understand the link between sleep and emotional well-being, emphasizing that getting good sleep is a personal responsibility over a lifetime. Try to keep daily charts of sleep habits and moods, preferably in collaboration with your child, so the connection becomes obvious. If you don't have time or energy for charts, consider keeping notes on your phone.

Goodnight, Mood

America is suffering a national epidemic of poor sleep, and adolescents are among the worst casualties. Adolescents with mood disorders suffer the most.

"Multilevel interventions are needed," says Wendy Troxel, a senior scientist and sleep expert at the RAND Corp., explaining that not just families but schools and state and local governments should help seek solutions.

Until our society gets smarter, however, there are several ways you can help improve your kids' sleep:

- Make sure first to get your child evaluated to see if any physical issue is interfering.
- Keep their bedrooms dark, cool, and quiet, with no computers or TVs. Insist that phones and laptops be used only in one central place in the home.
- Phones should be turned off and ideally handed to you one to two hours before bedtime.
- Buy a few old-fashioned alarm clocks rather than letting your kids use their phones.
- No alcohol before bedtime (and not before the legal drinking age of 21—they're adolescents!) Also, no caffeine or exercise within four hours of going to bed.

- Keep weekend bedtime hours within reasonable limits to avoid the "social jet lag" from waking early Monday after sleeping in on Sunday.
- Encourage your child to get plenty of exposure to natural light, ideally in the morning. Light cues the brain to kick-start our circadian rhythm. If that's not possible, try a sunlight lamp designed for people who suffer mood changes in the winter. (See also Chapter 3.)
- For insomnia, try two of your grandmother's remedies: a hot bath 90 minutes before bed, and a cup of cold or warm milk, which is rich in tryptophan, a sleep-inducing amino acid.
- Keep an eye on sleeplessness, which needs to be addressed right away. Good-quality sleep is essential to improving your child's mood—so important that your child's doctor may recommend temporary sleep aids such as Benadryl, melatonin, or low-dose trazodone, which are milder than other sleep medications and are not addictive. Be wary of using other medications for your child's sleep, because many can be habit-forming, and be sure to keep your own medications safely secured.

Nutrition

There is growing evidence that the way we eat can support or subvert our mental health. In fact, dietary guidelines from the US Department of Agriculture and the US Department of Health and Human Services now recommend healthy diets to prevent depression. A 2020 review of research suggests that the so-called Mediterranean diet, as well as similar regimes that include lots of fruit, vegetables, whole grains, fish, olive oil, and low-fat dairy products, may indeed prevent depression, or at least slow its progression and help in its management. Other evidence suggests that omega-3 fatty acids, contained in fish and some plants, have positive effects on clinical depression, including in people with bipolar disorder, although they don't seem to help with mania. (See our suggestions on supplements in Chapter 3.) Further study is needed to determine the benefits for children and adolescents.

In contrast, the typical American diet, involving lots of red meat, processed food, sugar, potatoes, and high-fat butter and milk, has been associated with an increased *risk* of depression. A plausible explanation is that bad nutrition can cause chronic inflammation, a potential contributor to mood disorders. Not incidentally, the typical American diet also contributes to obesity, which itself is linked to depression.

Alas, still other research has found that adolescents with symptoms of bipolar disorder and depression are generally less eager to engage in healthy behavior, such as following a healthy diet. But that's where you come in. Throw out the junk food: make sure to the extent you can that you have fresh fruit and other healthy foods around the house. If need be, pack lunches.

Weight Management

Obesity has become epidemic in the United States in recent decades, and the numbers continue to rise, including among youth. Since the 1970s, the percentage of children and adolescents affected by obesity has more than tripled. In 2017–2018, on average, an estimated 19.3% of US children and adolescents aged 2 to 19 years were obese. The numbers were alarmingly higher for racial minorities: more than 24% for Black children and nearly 26% for Latinos.

There's a chicken-and-egg relationship between being overweight and being depressed. One 2010 study found that obese people were at a 55% greater risk than others to become depressed during their lifetimes. At the same time, many depressed folk gain weight for reasons that can include low motivation to exercise and the side-effects of many medications.

Being overweight can lead to physical illnesses such as diabetes, sap self-esteem, and make kids targets for bullies. If this is a problem for your child, consider these suggestions:

- Be a good role model with what you eat and when. Many studies show that kids are influenced by their parents' behavior around food.
- As much as you're able, have lots of fresh produce and other healthy foods around, while limiting purchases of ice cream, soft drinks, candy, and processed snacks.
- Be careful how you talk about weight. Obviously avoid fat-shaming, nagging about diets, or ordering kids to eat every morsel on their plates.

Predictability

To best support your child's mental health, you'll want to make your home more safe, stable, warm, and emotionally supportive of all its members. We have several ideas for how to do this.

Safety First

An adolescent's brain develops rapidly, and within a few more years your child is almost sure to be less impulsive and more risk-averse. For now, however, you need to take precautions, especially considering that being depressed can make some young people reckless.

This is crucial: All parents, but especially parents of children with mood disorders, should keep any firearms in the home unloaded *and* under lock and key.

The American Foundation for Suicide Prevention (AFSP) recommends that the best way to help protect someone in distress is to "temporarily remove all lethal means, including firearms, from the home until the person is no longer in a state of crisis." It's illegal to store firearms in self-storage units, yet it's often possible to find local businesses and law enforcement agencies willing to take them temporarily. Students at Johns Hopkins University recently developed an online map of safe gun-storage facilities in Maryland. Options for storage vary by community and state, but they can be easily found by calling your local police department.

The odds of a young person dying by suicide are many times higher in homes where guns are present than in homes without guns. Of the nearly 2,400 children and adolescents aged 5 to 18 who died by suicide in the United States in 2018, 40% used a firearm. What's more, youth who use firearms for suicide tend to provide fewer warning signs leading up to their deaths than those who use other methods, implying that suicide by gunshot may often depend simply on access to a gun.

We assume that if you're reading this book, you are an exceptionally responsible parent, so please forgive what may seem like a no-brainer reminder: Kids suffering from depression should not have access to firearms—including for hunting or whatever other hobby may involve them. Later, maybe, but this isn't the right time.

Authoritarian Versus Authoritative

Abundant research confirms that the most effective parenting style to support mental health is neither the once-popular "authoritarian" (or dictatorial) method nor the recently appealing "permissive" (laissez-faire) one, but rather, a more nuanced, "authoritative" style, that is nurturing, warm, and flexible, but doesn't back down. (One of the best arguments for a warm parental style is research showing that children who grow up in poverty are two to three times more likely than others to develop mental health problems, but that a mother's emotional support can reduce those odds. While it hasn't been specifically researched, we suspect that a father's support can also do so.)

Authoritative parents set clear limits on behavior. They may listen to a child's viewpoint, but don't always accept it. Say a daughter is caught having shoplifted mascara. An authoritarian parent may yell or spank, while a "permissive" parent may accept the daughter's excuses. The authoritative parent will take time to explain why stealing is wrong, and find a disciplinary strategy that conveys a lesson, such as taking the girl to return the mascara and apologize to the store owner.

In the best-case scenario, you began setting clear rules and even assigning chores for your children long before they started questioning everything you say. The younger kids are when they first understand your expectations, the more likely they will rise to them. Still, firm limits are worth setting and maintaining even with feisty adolescents.

Chamique Holdsclaw remembers the shock of moving from her parents' middle-class apartment in Queens to her grandmother's public-housing apartment—in the same borough, but a world away. "I had so much freedom when I was living with my parents that I'm glad nothing bad happened to me," she recalls, laughing. "At just 9 or 10 my friends and I knew the subway system like the back of our hands. But my grandmother's discipline and structure really hit hard. She never let me hang around outside, unless it was church or volunteer work. Although she did let me play on a basketball court that was right outside her window, so she could watch me." Holdsclaw soon learned how good it felt to get exercise, develop a skill, and join a team. The rest, of course, is history.

Many parents find it helps to write down the most important family rules and post them in a prominent place, such as taped on the refrigerator. Among other things, this holds you accountable for enforcing them. You may also want to draw up a behavior contract for your children to sign. This would specify both rules—such as evening curfew times and limits on screen time—and consequences for breaking them. Don't have too many rules, however—the more you have, the greater the risk they'll be broken—and try to focus more on positive reinforcement than punishment. Catching your child being good is a powerful motivator. The great psychologist William James said, "The deepest principle in human nature is the craving to be appreciated." Make the effort to find and remark on something your child is doing right— even little things like getting up on time or being nice to a sibling.

If you must dole out the discipline, make it fit the crime. If your child has found something he or she truly loves, like going to the gym or spending time with a friend, you may be tempted to take that away in response to bad behavior. Find an alternative. If, as we assume, your overriding goal is helping your kid stay sane, the last thing you want to do is take away what may be his or her few sources of joy.

Communication 101

As a parent, what you say and how you say it can have a powerful effect. You have the opportunity not only to express your love and expectations but, ideally, also to offer alternatives for the hostile language in your child's head.

The psychologist John Duffy, who writes advice books for raising teens, suggests that parents maintain an "emotional bank account": the savings of trust and warmth and happy memories that sustain you through challenging times. Remember that your routine communication is the hard currency of your relationship. Pay attention especially to the ratio of positive to negative feedback you deliver.

A Denial-Free Zone

While considering how you talk with your child, think also about how you talk to *yourself.* Many parents reasonably wish their children weren't suffering and that life could return to normal, ASAP. Supporting these hopes is the often-intermittent nature of the child's depression, with sometimes long periods when everything seems fine. But then comes the next emergency, leaving everyone surprised and unprepared, without a safety net. Far better to avoid wishful thinking and make a plan that you'll follow faithfully from the first evidence that there's a serious problem.

Once your child is diagnosed, model forthrightness. Talk calmly but frankly about emotions, acknowledging them without nagging. One mother says that every few days she'll ask her 13-year-old son, "How's your mood?" It's been a helpful invitation not only for her child to talk about anything bothering him but to consider how moods are always changing and are separate from his permanent identity.

One of the best things a parent can do for a depressed child is to be open about his or her own emotional struggles. In the early 1980s, Harvard psychiatrist William Beardslee developed an intervention called "Family Talk," based on the understanding that a parent's depression is a major risk factor for depression in a child. In the formal program, a clinician meets with the family over several sessions to help improve the way the family communicates. But families can also try the approach informally by meeting together and talking frankly about depression as a biological illness that can be managed with insight and care. Small studies suggest "Family Talk" has long-lasting benefits for children.

Such honest conversations are not always easy. It's important to avoid oversharing. Some kids may be made more depressed by parents who suggest the kids should be taking care of *them*. It's especially risky if you're fighting with your partner and one or both of you craves support from the children. No matter what your situation is, you need to set clear boundaries, with no ambivalence about who is the child in the relationship. If you choose to open up, carefully consider the potential impact on your child. For example, it's best not to talk about any suicidal impulses you've had. A good basic script is: "I know it's hard to ask for help. There was a point in my life when I also needed help, but once I got it, it worked. As your mom (or dad), I want the same for you, and it's my job to help you get it."

Try not to let on how anxious you may be about your child's struggles with depression, but don't hide or downplay the truth. Your adolescent already knows something is wrong, and if kept in the dark, he or she may decide the situation is bleaker than it is. By comparison, the truth can be reassuring. There's an illness, but it's eminently treatable.

> "We have been completely open about depression," says Maria. "Lourdes understands that it might never go away, but she also knows she has her psychiatrist and a therapist as part of her support team. She knows that medication is an available option should it be needed. We want her to learn to take ownership of her care and know that it is manageable."

The Art of Being Available

Most adolescents are starting to separate from their parents, sharing less of themselves and their feelings. For a child with depression, shame and despair may increase that reluctance to confide. There's an art to letting them know, without hovering, that you'll be there when they need to talk, that you'll respect their privacy, take them seriously, and avoid judging them. Try not to give your anxiety the upper hand. Listen more than you talk, and don't always try to "fix" things. Three powerful words to remember are "Tell me more!"—but only when the time is right.

Many parents say it's easiest to talk while driving somewhere together, which doesn't entail eye contact. Put away the cellphone and turn down the music. For your icebreaker, avoid pat questions like "How was your day?" which may elicit little more than a grunt. Be strategic about mining positive emotions. If your kid likes working on computers, ask for technological advice. If he's merely watching TV or reading, ask what he likes about a favorite show or book.

A car in motion is often the best setting for sensitive topics such as drugs and alcohol, sex, or depression itself. You might broach the topic by asking what *other* kids at school are doing. If your child shares a mistake, make it clear that your love won't disappear even if you dislike the behavior.

To add to your family's emotional bank account, find pleasurable ways to spend time together, away from screens. Repeated studies, including one 2016 survey of 8,500 US students, have found that sharing family meals can reduce the risk of depression, particularly for girls. To be sure, it's not easy to maintain rituals when family members keep different schedules, and especially when a child with a mood disorder threatens to make each meal a disaster. Often you may feel you're plugging away without any sign of progress. But plug away you must; it's your best investment in a healthier future.

Being There When Your Child Is LGBTQ+

Times have changed a lot since the relatively recent past, when many kids with differing sexual identities stayed mum about them until long after they left home. Today there are abundant resources, online and in school, to support youth in understanding their sexual identities. This is a change that could not have come too soon.

In 2018, a British study based on interviews with 4,800 youths found that lesbian, gay, and bisexual youth between the ages of 16 and 21 were four times more likely to have felt depressed, harmed themselves, and thought about suicide. The causes included bullying and stigma related to their sexuality.

"Both gender and sexuality have been constant points of confusion for me for at least two years now," says Andy,

18, who believes this may have been a contributor to his cutting himself. "I wear makeup nearly every day, wore a long flowing dress to homecoming, paint my nails—all generally feminine things."

Other research has pointed out the obvious: Families' attitudes can have a huge impact on their LGBTQ+ or otherwise sexually nonconforming children's mental and physical health. LGBTQ+ youth from highly rejecting families are more than eight times more likely to try to take their lives as young adults. They are also nearly six times as likely to report being depressed and roughly three times as likely to take illegal drugs. You may feel uncomfortable and even disappointed to learn that your child is not cisgender. We strongly advise you to consider these statistics before you react. Even encouraging your child to keep his or her sexual identity a secret can be harmful. It may take some emotional work for you to accept this unexpected development, but think of it as an investment in your child's safety. Show them you still love them; advocate for them if they are mistreated, and require other family members to show respect. Ideally, you'll also find a way to connect your child with an LGBTQ+ role model.

> "I don't have any gripe with how either of them handles my being non-binary, even though I know it's confusing for them," Andy says of his parents. "They'll probably always call me by the name they gave me and they'll always use he/him for me, but if I asked them I think they'd make a valid effort to change how they see me. My parents are both fairly progressive and accepting of changing social norms, and I love that about them."

Break It Down

Depression often causes problems with thinking and understanding. Emotional stress may make it hard for your son or daughter to process what you're saying. Pay attention to your expectations, which may be unrealistic.

> "My son's school psychologist noticed that he wasn't clearly identifying his feelings," says Stephanie, whose son's depression began in the fourth grade. "He would say things like 'I feel red.' So we worked together with the school to help him identify and expand his vocabulary for feelings. It wasn't just mad, sad, and happy. It was words like frustrated, vulnerable, disappointed, etc. Once we helped him with that, he was able to empathize with *us* when we described what we were feeling in reaction to his depression."

Your child may be able to speak four languages and solve advanced calculus problems in his or her head, but until the symptoms of depression subside, don't expect mature or even particularly coherent reactions. Maybe tonight's homework shouldn't be the first priority. Maybe you'll need to muster extra patience with what might seem like the simplest of transitions, such as getting ready for school.

Problem-Solving

No one expects you to be your child's therapist, but you can step in occasionally as a cognitive coach. Help your son or daughter understand that the first step toward solving a problem is to define it. Subsequently, you can brainstorm together about possible solutions, considering the pros and cons of each option, until your child is ready to choose.

Jane Gillham, a clinical psychologist at Swarthmore College, says parents can help their kids by expressing the way their own moods might influence their thinking, and even whether they sometimes "catastrophize." "When you catch yourself jumping to a conclusion, point it out. Then talk through the process of evaluating not only the worst-case scenario but also the best case and most likely case. Children often learn by imitating those they admire. By modeling the process of evaluating your own thinking, weighing the evidence, and correcting the inaccuracies, you can help them learn these essential skills."

If your son or daughter shares a thought that seems unrealistically pessimistic, you can gently make that clear. Let's say your child is talking about a temporary problem as if it will never end. You might say something like: "I know this is really hard right now, but let's think about how you've gotten through similar situations."

Talking—or Not—to Others

If your child confides in you, be sensitive about how you use the information. There will be times when you need to reach out to others, including other parents, for advice or support, and there are also people, such as teachers, who have a legitimate reason to know what's going on in your child's life. But talk to your child first. If he or she strongly prefers that you not discuss the problems with a certain person—such as a family friend, a favorite aunt, or another sibling—ask yourself whether this other party really needs to be informed. If you do go ahead, prevail on the person to keep the information confidential, and as a rule don't include any sensitive information in emails or texts that can be forwarded.

It Takes a Family

A big part of your work in creating a safe and predictable home is getting every member on board with your plans and strategies.

> Charlene, who has two children with mood disorders, learned this the hard way. "I parent one way; my husband parents another. He's the one who makes the rules and sticks with them. I'm the one who's around the kids more, and they wear me down, so I give in. I think sometimes my husband is too hard on the kids. He thinks I'm too lenient." The mixed signals made their home life chaotic, she says, until she learned: "I thought I was being kinder, but what they really needed was consistency." A family counselor helped the couple resolve their differences and present a more unified front.

To stay on the same page, you and your partner may need to do some work on your own relationship. Coping with the physical, emotional, and financial demands of raising a depressed adolescent could stress any couple. Although some relationships don't survive, others find that the challenge brings them closer, providing a sense of shared purpose. Couples who've endured credit their success to simple, familiar rules applicable to any well-functioning family. They say they prioritize their marriage, putting each other first and not allowing their children to play them off against each other. They are open about their differences, but find ways to cooperate. They are self-aware enough to notice how they react to each other when reacting to their kids. And if needed—as is often the case when raising children with issues—they get couples' therapy.

> "I started to recognize how the less emotional he got, the more I got," says Charlene, referring to her husband, Ted. "So pretty soon I became this huge ball of emotions. I had to work on that, just like he had to work on his withdrawing."

Parenting without a partner raises a different set of issues. You may need to accept you need more help than you're getting. Don't be shy about leaning on extended family and close friends for emotional support and practical help. If they aren't available, try to find a mentor who can develop a lasting relationship with your child and give you at least a few free hours a day. Look into Big Brothers Big Sisters, the largest US mentoring nonprofit, or see if you can hire a local college student—perhaps someone studying psychology.

> "You need a support network," says Sara, who raised four children with different mood disorders by herself for several years. "My family lives up in Canada, so family was out for me. But I have a lot of very good friends. Some of them would come over and sit with the kids from time to time—even for a few hours once a month. That let me get out occasionally and it really made a big difference."

Siblings: The Good, Bad, and Ugly

In the best of families, siblings compete for the limited resource of their parents' attention. They can genuinely love each other and get along most of the time but still tally points and constantly compare. This is one of the most basic evolutionary instincts, a force larger than any of our best intentions. It may add an extra burden if one or more of your children is coping with depression.

Brothers and sisters may bear the brunt of a sibling's angry and even violent behavior. They may mourn the loss of the close connection they once shared with that sibling and long for a more "normal" family life. Often they get lost in the commotion as parents cope with consecutive crises. Some families finally see their depressed child improve, only to plunge into new chaos with a sibling who has seemed to be biding time to make a bid for attention.

Once again, communication is key. As soon as younger children can understand, explain in simple terms what your child with depression is going through. Often a sibling will wrongly assume that his or her brother or sister can control the behavior.

> "I've had many talks with my younger son about how he'd be a lot more empathetic if his brother was in a wheelchair," says Beth. "To be honest, I don't think they've helped. My only hope is that years from now it may make sense, and maybe then they can have a relationship. I hope I'm still alive to enjoy it!"

Everyone reacts differently. Some brothers and sisters of a sibling with serious depression withdraw from family life. Some may throw themselves into schoolwork and extracurricular pursuits in hopes of staying out of the house as much as possible, or of simply establishing themselves as "normal."

Keep alert to subtle provocative behavior by the ostensibly better-behaving sibling toward the child who is struggling with depression.

"My younger son would whisper insults like 'loser!' which at first I didn't hear, but which would always cause my older son to explode," says Beth. "He was very crafty about trying to make himself look like the angel versus his brother, the devil. Once I realized what was going on, I talked to both of them explicitly about it and started handing out consequences when he did that."

Few parents intend to neglect their children. Yet when you're feeling overburdened and exhausted, it's easy to take the path of least resistance. Unfortunately, allowing yourself to be swept along by events means you'll be pulled more toward the child with the problem and away from those who aren't as obviously demanding. It takes effort to notice and correct this tendency. Try, if you can, to set aside some daily one-on-one time with each child. Also try to avoid having different rules for different children—even though sometimes you must.

One mother says that when her 14-year-old daughter was at the low point of a depressive episode, "I didn't make her do chores, because she couldn't have done them." This unsurprisingly didn't delight that child's 13-year-old younger sister, who was still expected to step up.

In this situation, it may help to have a frank talk with the unhappy sibling. Explain that you're not showing favoritism. You're treating each child similarly by individualizing the rules for each based on differing capacities. After all, younger children aren't expected to do the same chores as older ones, but they're still expected to do tasks appropriate for their age and ability.

Strength

The Art of Bouncing Back

If you've read even one recent parenting book or attended a single recent meeting at your child's school, you've undoubtedly heard the modern buzzwords "resilience" and "grit." They're trendy for good reasons. Both connote the vital ability to adapt to stressful life events and bounce back from adversity: especially important goals for a child who is coping with depression.

A major ingredient of grit is simple optimism. It's not enough to ward off depression, but it can reduce the severity of the symptoms. A 2011 Australian study suggested a high level of optimism in adolescents cuts the risk of depression by half.

Everything we've already told you in this chapter about communication, problem-solving, and family cohesiveness can help create a more optimistic child. Some research suggests that mindfulness can also help, particularly when it is focused on developing a sense of gratitude. Just as a brain can get increasingly adept at depression, it can also get into a habit of being more positive. There are many ways to practice this art, from a meditation class to writing a letter of thanks to someone, to confiding in a journal, to simply taking time each evening to name three things that went well. Don't wait for Thanksgiving, in other words. Without trying to force a change of feelings or deny the reality of an illness, find ways to talk about gratitude with your kids. If keeping a journal is a stretch, you might want to take a walk together with your phones and photograph things that make you happy.

"I Can Do It!"

"Self-efficacy" is the formal term for people's faith in their ability to perform well in a particular situation. People with high self-efficacy believe they can achieve results they desire through their own efforts. The concept is closely linked to optimism and has been associated with a decreased risk of depression in young people. You can do a lot to help build a sense of self-efficacy. Get to know your child's strengths, weaknesses, and motivations. Give honest (but not overcritical) feedback. Provide as many opportunities as you can to explore new pursuits and sharpen skills. (You can often find inexpensive classes at your local community center.) Look for challenges that aren't overwhelmingly hard but that still reward effort. A part-time job can go far in that direction, with rewards expressed explicitly on the monthly paycheck.

This may take some cajoling, at least at first. There's nothing like depression to sap interest in trying new things. Yet that first step out can often be enough of a reward to keep going. That's why "behavioral activation"—getting someone to take that first hard step—is considered a therapy in itself.

The whole family may need to participate, at least at first, to fight the inertia. If you notice your partner and kids sitting around on a Saturday, staring at their screens, try pulling everyone away for a walk, a board game, or merely a good conversation.

Kelly Lambert, a neuroscientist at the University of Richmond in Virginia, studies the rodent equivalent of optimism. In one of her experiments, she observed two groups of rats: one that had to dig in the dirt to find tasty Froot Loops ("worker rats") and another that was simply given them ("trust-fund rats"). Subsequently, Lambert presented both groups with a problem-solving challenge: a little ball with a Froot Loop inside it. The worker rats worked harder and longer to get at the Froot Loop, a result Lambert calls "learned persistence."

Lambert is such an advocate of this approach to combat depression that she has coined the term "behaviorceuticals" to convey the idea that some behaviors may be as powerful as pharmaceuticals. "Physical exercise is great but seeing a direct result of our effort when we engage in certain tasks or hobbies can build both emotional resilience and self-efficacy," she says, adding: "The worker rats have healthier stress hormone profiles, a characteristic that protects against the emergence of depressive symptoms. These effort-based rewards likely served as our ancestors' 'prehistoric Prozac'—keeping them foraging and hunting for that next dose of mood-boosting neurochemicals."

Of course there are all kinds of differences between humans and rodents! But the basic structures and chemical workings of our brains are surprisingly similar, which is why scientists so often pick rats and mice as stand-ins.

One mother recalled how her depressed teenager's mood lifted after she helped teach him to drive, step by step. Prizing independence, like most teens, he had a powerful incentive to learn. "I drove him every day at first until he was comfortable with the route," said his mom. "Then he drove himself, and I followed in my car until he got comfortable with that. And then finally, he was ready to go on his own."

Think Bigger

Another potential countervailing force to depression that your own mother may have mentioned is to think more about other people. This isn't something we'd encourage you to suggest to a child in the depths of depression. But it's a habit that is certainly worth cultivating. Researchers have found strong links between altruistic behavior and emotional health. A 2021 study of brain scans of 72 adults who were genetically at high risk for depression suggested altruistic feelings protect against depressive symptoms. Maybe your child can begin by caring for a pet dog or cat. It's fine to start small, and many parents have told us that introducing a four-legged friend was one of their best moves. Additionally, churches and synagogues often organize volunteer programs you can participate in as a family.

> "I was so lucky that one of my son's high school teachers insisted the kids complete a number of hours in a local volunteer program," says Beth. "The sad truth is I probably wouldn't have been able to convince him myself. But because he needed to pass that class, he got involved in a project that helped teach kids in low-income neighborhoods about nutrition and exercise, and he not only enjoyed helping them, but got more interested in taking better care of himself."

Exercise and the Great Outdoors

We're guessing you've already heard about the mood-lifting benefits of simple exercise. The research that supports this is abundant and increasing. Harvard psychiatrist John Ratey, author of *Spark: The Revolutionary New Science of Exercise and the Brain*, compares exercise to a medicine cabinet full of natural stimulants and mood boosters, including the feel-good neurotransmitter serotonin and endorphins, the endogenous opioid hormones that relieve pain and anxiety. That's on top

of the other physical benefits of getting moving, such as helping you stay in shape—boosting self-esteem—and improving
sleep. For some depressed people, regular exercise works as
well as antidepressants, although it's probably not enough for
someone whose illness is severe.

Scientists have found that regular physical exercise even
helps improve nerve cell growth in the hippocampus, where
depressed people tend to have deficits. While your adolescent
may resist getting started, it only takes a little time to start
to feel a lot better, which can be self-enforcing. Talk up the
benefits of an after-school sports program. Offer bribes for the
first couple of weeks if you need to. If you can afford it, buy a
monthly gym membership. Or start taking walks or bike rides
together.

> "I was never an athletic kid—I had asthma attacks,"
> writes Ruby Walker, in her book about her depression
> as a teen. "When I heard that exercise could be good
> for mood disorders, I started walking around the neigh-
> borhood at sunset every couple of days. Not only did
> those walks help my brain make more endorphins, they
> also became my quiet time for reflection. I'd listen to
> music, feel the grass, watch the clouds, smell the flow-
> ers. Spending some time in nature helped me feel more
> real somehow."

Walker makes an additional evidence-based point, which is
that green environments can help improve moods. A 2014
study found that merely living in neighborhoods with higher
levels of green space was linked with significantly lower levels of depression, anxiety, and stress. If you don't have the

resources to live in such a neighborhood, try to find ways to spend time in parks or on trails.

> "I can date my son's recovery from depression from the time he started mountain-biking on weekends," says Meg. "He lost a ton of weight, made friends, and found something that seemed to define him."

Don't Forget the Love

It's vitally important to remember that however horribly your adolescent may be behaving during emotional turmoil, in all likelihood you remain at the center of his or her world.

The author Toni Morrison gives this advice: When your child walks into the room, your eyes should light up. When kids are causing trouble, voluntarily or not, it's so easy to meet their entrance with a weary or frustrated or critical face. But then you're just adding to the harsh soundtrack in their heads. Kids often feel they can "afford" to behave at their worst with their mother or father, yet even during a tirade may be seeking reassurance and affection.

We're not suggesting this won't take a lot of emotional energy. Don't forget to eat, sleep, exercise, and find occasional outdoor escapes of your own. In particularly difficult times, you may also need ways to remind yourself of how much you love your child. Keep a baby picture handy. You need to bring your A-game to this limited time when your kids are still young and in your care.

An interviewer asked Ruby Walker, "What can parents do if they believe their teen might be experiencing depression?" She responded:

> "Love them," she answered. "Depression can make people act in unpredictable or unsettling ways. When your

kid is acting out, spacing out, staying up, skipping class, snapping, hiding things, and generally being 'bad'—that is when they need love and compassion the most. Don't get them in trouble, offer them help. Let them know that your love is unconditional."

So now you have the script. We hope it will help you deal with the forbidding topics of the next chapter, namely sex, drugs, alcohol, and social media. These represent some of the toughest challenges for a parent of any adolescent, but especially one who is coping with depression.

Chapter Six

Sex, Drugs, and Social Media

Parenting by many measures has become more labor-intensive than ever. Overall, that's a good thing. The main reason the job is so much harder is because we *know* so much more.

Unlike our parents' parents, for instance, most Americans now understand that "spare the rod, spoil the child" is bad advice. Surveys show Millennials and Gen Z parents are spanking much less than their own folks did. What's more, contemporary moms and dads know that mental illness is real, that children aren't exempt, and that a wide variety of treatments can help make things better.

All of this implies a lot more emotional work for adults raising children. But there is also so much more to gain than ever before—including the chance to provide more effective support to our children as they embark on their adult lives. We also can hope for more honest and loving relationships with them, and maybe even a saner, more compassionate world. These are ideals you might keep in mind during some of the hardest times, which we predict will involve dealing with one or more of three vexing challenges: sex, drugs (and alcohol), and social media.

As with most other topics in this book, these are relevant hurdles for almost every parent of an adolescent yet become much more serious when your child has a mood disorder.

Below, we'll offer some evidence-based tips to cope with each of these dilemmas.

Starting With Sex

Sex remains a famously difficult topic for parents to discuss with their children, and vice versa. Yet discuss it you must. It will likely become an issue sooner than you expect.

Young people today are less sexually active than in previous decades, but quite a few of them are still hooking up. In 2019, more than 38% of high schoolers said they'd had sex, with more than 27% of teens reporting relations in the previous three months, according to the Centers for Disease Control and Prevention (CDC). Twelve percent reported they had not used any method to prevent pregnancy, and less than 10% had ever been tested for HIV.

While sex in a healthy and reasonably mature relationship can be a joy, you have reason to worry that loneliness and lack of self-esteem will drive your depressed child into dangerous liaisons. Depression not only makes sex more likely, and at an earlier-than-average age; it also makes it more dangerous. Depressed children can often be more reckless and impulsive than even your average adolescent, with consequently greater risk of unwanted pregnancy, sexually transmitted diseases (STDs), and heartbreak that can trigger self-harm.

Getting a diagnosis and sustained treatment is your best hope of helping your child develop more responsible behavior. We also hope that by now you've done enough work on your relationship to have open communication about delicate issues. Once those two conditions are met, the following suggestions may help you encourage healthy sexual behavior. You may be surprised to hear that most adolescents say they share their parents' values about sex and could use some encouragement in delaying it.

Think of this process as not one big talk, but a series of gentle check-ins that may go on over years:

Talking With Kids About Sex

- *Emphasize that you are not making moral judgments* but are concerned about your child's health, safety, and self-respect. Don't act like a know-it-all; it's okay to acknowledge this topic can be hard and confusing.
- *Talk about how to say no.* Schools have been doing a better job recently in teaching the basics of "consent," but it won't hurt to have a conversation to make sure it has sunk in. Help your child understand that you can't give consent when you are drunk or high.
- *Explain the dangers of "sexting,"* the receiving and sending of sexually explicit photos by text. You might be surprised by how many kids do it—more than 27% of those between 12 and 17 years old, according to one large analysis in 2018. Kids need to be reminded that once they send anything into the ether, they've lost control of it forever—and it may well survive on some website for years. The humiliation that follows errant texts could aggravate depression or even trigger suicidal thinking and/or behaviors like an attempt.

- *Meet your child's romantic partner*, and if possible also the partner's parents. And yes, this assumes you've done the work you need to do on your relationship with your child.
- *Even 12 years old is not too early to start talking about birth control.* The risks begin at puberty. Remember, you can't follow your kid around 24/7, so if your daughter says she needs it, as hard as that may be to imagine, it's probably better to help than not.
- *Let your child know that masturbation is healthy*, as long as it's done in private and not to the exclusion of everything else.
- *Enlist your child's doctor* to discuss the risks of sexual activity, and be sure to keep up regular prevention visits so that the doctor can establish an ongoing dialogue.

During Chamique Holdsclaw's high school years, she was often warned to take care not to get pregnant. But what made the biggest impression for her was when her grandmother helped her understand her own worth. "She would tell me, 'It's not where you're from. It's where you're going,'" Holdsclaw recalled. "And I never wanted to let her down."

Alcohol, Weed, and Pills

Another challenge for parents that becomes a lot harder when your child is depressed involves drinking and drugs. In the short term, getting buzzed or high can ward off symptoms of depression and anxiety. Over time, however, it makes them worse.

More than half of US kids will try drugs, with many able to avoid getting hooked. Yet kids with mood disorders of all kinds are at high risk of dangerous drug use, including addiction.

Other risks include unwanted pregnancies and STDs, school failure, trouble with police, injuries, accidents, and increased danger of suicide attempts. Alcohol and drugs can also sabotage antidepressants, preventing them from working or intensifying side-effects.

Booze

Adolescents on average are drinking less than they used to. Yet similarly to trends with sex, there's still a lot of drinking going on.

A 2019 CDC national survey of high school students found that in the previous month, nearly one-third had drunk alcohol, 14% had engaged in binge-drinking, and 17% had been in a car with a driver who had been drinking. And again, the risks are serious: Heavy alcohol use can lead not only to accidents and death but changes in brain development that may have lifelong impact, including future alcoholism.

Cannabis

While fewer adolescents are drinking, many more are using marijuana. Roughly 8% of eighth graders in a recent survey said they'd "vaped" at least once in the past year. And as you may have heard, this isn't your mother's marijuana. Today's weed is grown in ways that make it more potent, concentrating the active ingredient, tetrahydrocannabinol (THC), by at least three times as much as in years past. Compounding the danger is that marijuana has become much more prevalent and easier to obtain. As of this writing, it's legal for recreational use in 19 states plus Washington, DC, and permitted for medical use in over 35 others. Nowhere is marijuana legal for minors, yet that hasn't slowed down the consumption. A 2021 study of California youth found that teenagers' marijuana use climbed by 23% during the year after the drug was legalized for adults.

Vaping, "edibles," tinctures, and teas have made the drug more convenient to use and to hide from parents. Newish, synthetic marijuana-like drugs with names like "K2," "Fake Weed," "Legal Weed," and "Spice" are easily confused with marijuana but more dangerous to consume. Some cause increased heart rate and blood pressure, anxiety, vomiting, and even hallucinations.

Kids have been encouraged to believe that marijuana is safer than alcohol because it's "natural" and sanctioned for some adult medical problems. In a controversial trend, some doctors have even prescribed cannabis to minors, for complaints ranging from cancer to anxiety to attention-deficit/hyperactivity disorder (ADHD).

The Food and Drug Administration (FDA) has approved CBD (cannabidiol, the second most active ingredient in marijuana) to treat some forms of epilepsy in children. There are no other approved uses for minors—for good reason.

Experts believe that adolescents' developing brains are more vulnerable to marijuana's active ingredient, THC, which can disrupt attention, memory, and concentration. In the summer of 2021, researchers at the National Institutes of Health announced evidence of an additional danger. A survey of 280,000 young adults—aged 18 to 35—revealed a link between cannabis use and higher levels of suicidal thoughts, plans, and attempts. Moreover, note that even without THC, CBD can interfere with medications for depression.

While alcohol and marijuana are the most prevalent temptations, other potentially more dangerous drugs, including cocaine, methamphetamines, LSD, and MDMA (Ecstasy), are often disturbingly easy to obtain, even on high school

campuses. Another worrying trend is that of youth raid-
ing their parents' medicine cabinets for prescription drugs.
In "Skittles parties," guests throw pills such as Ambien and
Ativan in a circle and then consume handfuls of them.

Your Vigilance Is Needed

Adolescents' brains are remarkably "plastic"—flexible and
growing. An advantage of this is they can learn things, like
new languages, faster than their elders. Unfortunately they
also tend to progress more speedily from substance use to
addiction and sometimes to death by overdose. In recent years,
nearly 100,000 Americans a year have died that way.

In his books, blogs, and public speaking, the writer David
Sheff has described how he narrowly avoided that fate with
his son, who has bipolar disorder. Nic started smoking marijuana and drinking alcohol as a young teenager, and his use
quickly escalated. Soon he was smoking every day, drinking
to the point of passing out and trying more dangerous drugs.

> "It got to the point that his use nearly killed him at least a
> dozen times," Sheff wrote us. "I'm not exaggerating. There
> were a couple overdoses; he was in emergency rooms, and
> once an ER doctor told me that they were going to have
> to amputate Nic's arm because it had become infected
> from shooting heroin and meth. They saved his arm and
> he did better for a while, but he relapsed and overdosed
> again. He was about 25 then. This time an ER doctor
> called and said, 'Mr. Sheff, you'd better get down here. We
> have your son. We don't know if he's going to make it.'"

Nic Sheff's story illustrates both the high risk of addiction for
kids with mental illness and the difficulty many parents face

in getting an accurate diagnosis. Over a decade of coping with his son's addiction, Sheff says, he got him into half a dozen different outpatient and residential treatment programs with many different specialists before a psychiatrist asked to see Nic's psychological testing. Sheff said there hadn't been any. Incredulous, the doctor ordered further evaluation which for the first time showed that Nic had bipolar disorder. His father believes that diagnosis—and subsequent treatment—saved his life.

Sheff, who went on to create a fund to support anti-addiction programs, warns other parents: Don't ever normalize drug use.

> Once, after Nic was caught with weed at high school, a counselor told his father: "Nic's a great kid. He's smart. He has lots of friends. He's a good athlete. Lots of kids use drugs—they're experimenting, partying. Nic will be fine," David says. "Nic wasn't fine. What the counselor should have said is that kids use drugs for reasons. We have to do what we can to find those reasons. If I'd found a psychiatrist or psychologist then who could have diagnosed Nic's mental illnesses, it's conceivable that we could have nipped his use in the bud. He believes and I believe it never would have escalated the way it did. I learned that we—parents, teachers, others who work with kids—can't accept drug use as a norm and harmless. We shouldn't assume it's not that big a deal and there's nothing we can do. There's a lot we can do."

Some parents end up in the frightening position of having to care for a child who is tripping on hallucinogens or has intentionally or unintentionally overdosed. If you're worried about your child taking dangerous substances or getting dependent on alcohol or marijuana, you should not hesitate to intervene, including exploring (with your doctor) drug testing and out-patient programs that provide intensive therapy sessions.

The following tips may also help:

• Communicate, communicate, communicate.

Tell your child in advance that you want to talk about drug use—not because he or she is in trouble but because it's time. Then make sure to listen carefully; don't interrupt or conde-scend. This is a question of health and safety.

It's your choice as to whether to disclose your own past drug use. But if you do, use caution, ask for advice from a trusted source, such as your child's doctor, and don't minimize the risks for still-developing brains.

> When Cindy's mother, Julie, talks to her about drugs, she emphasizes the risk of being publicly humiliated: a surefire way to get a teenage girl's attention. "Cindy is so rebellious that I know she's going to do what she's going to do," says her mom. "So I've tried to coach her about moderation and caution. I've told her lots of stories about friends of mine who've gotten into trouble. One was photographed vomiting at a party. This was before the internet, but she still had trouble living it down."

• Remember the no-brainers.

Lock up or throw out any unused dangerous substances such as narcotics or stimulants that may have been prescribed for a family member but are no longer needed. Lock up or carefully hide those still in use. Many a parent has learned this lesson the hard way and to lasting regret.

The most responsible way to get rid of such medications is to take them back to the pharmacy or see if your local law enforcement collects them. (You can search online for Drug Enforcement Agency guidelines.) If you must throw them in the trash, make sure the garbage isn't accessible to animals or children.

- Be the best possible role model.

Adolescent drinking appears to rise and fall along with drinking by adults in the same household—and even in the same community. We advise not giving your child alcohol until at least they reach the legal age of 21. Some parents think if it's in the home, it doesn't count. It does, and it sets a precedent.

- Talk about safety.

Remind your child never to drink anything he or she hasn't opened, or from a cup left out of sight for any amount of time. And obviously, no pills.

- Don't hesitate to set clear rules.

That doesn't mean they won't be broken, but studies show that on average your child will be less likely to get into serious trouble if your expectations are clear. You may also want to press home the possible consequences of getting caught at school, which might include getting suspended, or kicked off a sports team, or even sent to juvenile hall.

> "When I was growing up, I told my dad I wanted to try LSD," says Sally, a formerly depressed teenager who became a successful psychiatrist and mother. "He said, "Let's look into it; let's research it, and if it looks like it's really safe, I'll try it with you." They did, and Sally learned enough to discourage her from taking the trip.

- Ask pointed questions.

If your adolescent is going to a party, don't hesitate to ask where it is and whether there will be adult supervision. Don't be shy about checking with the adults who are supposedly in charge.

- Consider an "amnesty" policy.

A blogger for the Child Mind Institute suggests this idea: If your adolescent gets in trouble, he or she can call you and be honest about what's going on without the normal consequences for breaking rules. For instance, your child can call you from a party, if he or she has been drinking, and ask for a ride or an Uber rather than drive. It doesn't mean you won't have a frank talk the next morning; you're just prioritizing their safety.

- Prepare for emergencies.

If you suspect your child is using opioids, equip yourself with naloxone in case of an overdose. Keep it in your car, purse, or pocket. It's easy to use, as much as we hope you won't ever have to use it.

Yellow Flags

The American Academy of Child and Adolescent Psychiatry (AACAP) provides a list of warning signs that your child might be using marijuana:

- Acting silly and out of character for no reason
- Hanging out with a new group of friends who seem like they might be using
- Using new words such as "420" (slang for cannabis consumption), "dabbing" (a dance move resembling sneezing after smoking weed), and "shatter" (a cannabis extract)

- Being more irritable
- Losing interest in and motivation to do usual activities
- Falling asleep in class or at the dinner table
- Having trouble remembering things that just happened
- Coming home with red eyes and/or urges to eat outside of usual mealtimes
- Stealing money or having money that cannot be accounted for

The Addictive, Inevitable e-Universe

If your son or daughter is like the vast majority of youth in the internet age, he or she is spending several hours a day in virtual life: on computers and smartphones, texting away or immersed in social media. (In one survey, more than 90% of middle schoolers had their own smartphone and nearly three-quarters of them had started using Instagram or Snapchat.)

Maybe you're doing the same. We don't mean to judge, but we do want to alert you to the influence you'll have on everyone around you. This sort of behavior is highly contagious.

After all, not only is the internet not going away anytime soon, it offers advantages particularly well-suited for adolescents with depression. Social media can help withdrawn kids find friends, connecting them to "peeps" who share the same interests but might be shy or live far away. Social media can also nurture budding hobbies and interests; kids have used it to learn to play guitar, follow favorite musicians, or join a group of environmental activists—all without having to drive anywhere. Kids with mood disorders have also been able to educate themselves about their illness, in private, and find online support without stigma. Furthermore, while remote learning was far from ideal, it nonetheless saved millions of students from falling behind more than they would have during COVID-19.

All that said, it's no coincidence that the spectacular growth of social media ever since Facebook was founded in 2004 has coincided with the rapid growth in adolescent depression—and possibly also the suicide rate.

"Young people are bombarded with messages through the media and popular culture that erode their sense of self-worth—telling them they are not good-looking enough, popular enough, smart enough or rich enough," US Surgeon General Vivek Murthy wrote in his 2021 report on the adolescent mental health crisis.

Many experts believe that time spent with online "friends" does little to establish a sense of connection and in fact increases loneliness that can be a key factor in depression. In fact, levels of happiness in the United States have declined over the years that internet use has increased.

In 2018, the American Psychiatric Association (APA) found a clear link between social media use and adolescent depression. "Negative online exposure can have detrimental effects on the physical and mental health of teenagers," the APA warned, "causing depression, anxiety, increased suicidal thoughts, and even reports of completed teen suicide."

To be sure, there's a lot to unpack in the phrase "negative online exposure." We don't yet know precisely how spending time online might be adding to the rise in depression, but there are many reasonable theories. Adolescents with depression are particularly vulnerable to digital dangers that include online predators, cyberbullying, addiction to the exclusion of healthier pursuits, sleep deprivation, online humiliation and/or legal problems after impulsive oversharing, and exposure to a range of toxic content, including pornography and violence.

In 2021, former Facebook manager Frances Haugen drew global attention to the harm Facebook causes to young people's mental health. Haugen leaked thousands of internal documents to the *Wall Street Journal*, following up with hours of explosive testimony before Congress. In particular, she faulted Facebook for enabling "cyberbullying," which she said was extra-hurtful in that it followed children home after school. All too often, she said, the last thing children absorb before going to sleep is someone being cruel to them. She also described how girls are often led by Facebook's algorithm from content about diets to sites that encourage anorexia, a common coexisting condition of depression. "What's super tragic is Facebook's own research says as these young women begin to consume this eating disorder content, they get more and more depressed," she said, even as they're using the app more often.

The *Wall Street Journal's* lengthy exposé even hinted at a link between the rise in adolescent suicides and increasing use of Facebook, citing surveys that showed that among teenagers who reported suicidal thoughts, "13 percent of British users and 6 percent of American users traced the desire to kill themselves to Instagram." (Facebook has responded that "no single study is going to be conclusive.")

Social Media, the Internet, and Suicide

As much as we may love the convenience of smartphones and near-constant connectivity with our social networks, unfortunately the internet can present considerable dangers to vulnerable minds and lives. Websites exist that offer information on how to attempt suicide, and these draw an alarming number of page views per month. Evidence indicates that most people who view these sites are 30 or under and have struggled with mental health issues. Several European nations have managed to restrict access to certain of these sites, but so far the United States has lagged behind.

Challenging as it may be, it is important that you know what your child is doing online. It is important to talk directly and honestly with your teenager about their online use and to explain your concerns for their privacy and safety. For instance, make sure they know not to share their location or personal information. Let them know that you are available to review content with them if they have questions and/or worries. Educate them on trusted sources of health and other medical information. You might also consider, as part of the privilege of "phone ownership," explaining that you expect to be able to use parental controls, or that you may need to review content on your teen's phone (with their involvement). It is also helpful to keep screens and devices in a visible location in your home, where you can monitor what your child is up to and the amount of time they spend engaged in various activities online.

TMI

There's no question that kids all over the world are feeling depressed by the 24-7 drumbeat of bad news online. In particular, the looming existential threat from climate change has led to shocking rates of pessimism. In a 2022 survey of 10,000 people aged 16 to 25, living in 10 countries, three-quarters said "the future is frightening," and 56% said "humanity is doomed."

"Why Should I Study for a Future I Won't Have?" read a sign carried by high school sophomore Sophie Kaplan, who joined a protest march in 2020. "I don't understand why

I should be in school if the world is burning," Kaplan told a reporter. "What's the point of working on my education if we don't deal with this first?"

Such sentiments reverberate on social media (there's even an Instagram site called greenmemesfordepressedteens), while smartphones ping their anxious owners with updates on melting glaciers and burning forests. "Kids tell me they see such little hope," says Brian, a high school teacher in California.

This is a typical internet conundrum. Our increasing, constant online connections make us more informed than ever, which is positive to the extent that we can act on that knowledge but negative to the degree that we feel helpless. Talk to your kids often about how they feel about what they're reading and hearing in the news, and whenever possible, think of things they can do to counter despair. If they'll tolerate your company, you may even want to join with them to register voters or write postcards to Congress. Fred Rogers has recalled his own mother's advice when he was young and would see scary things in the news. "Look for the helpers," she would say. "You will always find people who are helping.'"

Mental Illness FOMO?

Here's a different sort of digital conundrum. As we've noted, social media has helped conquer much of the stigma surrounding mental illness, by disseminating stories of famous, successful people acknowledging their struggles and in general normalizing the topic. (At this writing, the Twitter hashtag #mentalillness had more than 1.7 billion videos.)

Yet we wonder if sometimes this benefit can turn into a problem, making depression seem more attractive, and even reinforcing symptoms through contagion. While we've yet to see research about this, many school faculty members and parents suspect it's true.

> "Kids are definitely googling to see if there's a diagnosis that fits their symptoms," says Katrina Southard, LCSW, coordinator of the Wellness Center at Archie Williams High School in San Anselmo, California. "I've had several recently wonder whether they have mental health disorders, including 'derealization,' which can occasionally rise to the level of being a disorder, but in most cases can be a normal part of being a teenager. I can't imagine they would have done this to this degree in the past without the ability to seek out a quick diagnosis."

A contributing trend is the "neurodiversity" movement, which often endorses the message that mental conditions commonly seen as disorders, such as ADHD and autism, are normal variations in the human genome, and in fact can be strengths. We applaud positive thinking—as long as it doesn't interfere with taking responsibility and, if need be, seeking treatment for genuine suffering.

What's a Parent to Do?

Parents of kids with depression need to be extra-vigilant about online dangers. You'll be walking a fine line, to be sure. Kids depend on the internet for schoolwork, socializing, and, increasingly, for establishing their autonomy and identity. You have to give them their space there, especially as they get older. Yet if your child is already emotionally fragile, you can't afford to tune out. At minimum we recommend you get familiar with some of the basics of social media, and observe where your kids are spending all that time. You wouldn't let them go to a bar at their age, or invite total strangers into your home, so consider this cautionary tale.

> Charlene's 15-year-old daughter Ellen loved Korean pop, and followed a few K-pop groups online. As she later told her mother, she found the site of a fan, a high school junior, who had discovered that one of the stars lost weight by eating just one sweet potato and an apple each day. Pretty soon Ellen started insisting on doing the same. It was the origin of her eating disorder.

The moral of the story is that you shouldn't wait to talk to your kids about what they're reading online, and also check out the sites yourself. Once again, communication is key. Don't assume your children understand the importance of privacy, and how easily whatever they post can be shared, and make sure they're aware of how different online activities make them feel. With inherently anti-authoritarian teens, sometimes the argument that works best is getting them to notice when and how they're being manipulated by large corporations.

Don't assume you can solve this problem with blanket decrees. One of the most bedeviling things for parents about the internet is that kids are constantly figuring out new ways to get around parental and other controls. For instance, even though a national law, the Children's Online Privacy Protection Act, prohibits companies from collecting online data from children under 13, many kids simply lie about their age.

Anyone with a smartphone understands the temptation to use it for distractions. Social media hook users with the mental stimulation of interesting news and "likes." A parent can easily feel powerless against such elemental forces, but remember: Silicon Valley moguls like Bill Gates and Steve Jobs have been some of the biggest sticklers in limiting their kids' screen time. Consider following their lead.

1. Be a Good Role Model

You can count on your children to watch what you do more closely than they listen to what you say. Be present with your family, limiting your own screen time. And don't undermine yourself by doing things like texting your children in school after you've told them not to text while at school. Again, consider what the inventors and sellers of these technologies have been doing in their own homes. Some Silicon Valley leaders have reportedly even required their children's child-care providers to sign contracts promising they won't use their phones in front of the kids.

Being a good role model may also mean taking a break from the news and talking about why you're doing so. You might also talk to your kids about how to distinguish fact from fiction.

2. Hold Out for as Long as You Can

Maybe your child shouldn't be the last one in her class to get a phone, but she sure shouldn't be the first. "Children 12 and under should not be on social media," Jean M. Twenge, a professor of psychology at San Diego State University and the author of *iGen*, a book about youth and technology, told the *New York Times*. Bill Gates reportedly didn't give his kids phones until they were 14 and subsequently limited their time with them. The Waldorf School of the Peninsula, based near Google's Mountain View campus, and a popular choice for many Silicon Valley parents, believes that exposing preteens to technology "can hamper their ability to fully develop strong bodies, healthy habits of discipline and self-control, fluency with creative and artistic expression, and flexible and agile minds."

Check out "Wait until Eighth," a savvy movement encouraging parents to join together to wait until eighth grade to give kids a smartphone.

In the meantime, ask your kids' school if they have a digital-citizenship class, and if they don't, why not?

3. Set Limits

You're paying the phone bill, right? There's increasing evidence that establishing limits is one of the healthiest things you can do for your child. Research published in *JAMA Pediatrics* has found that children get more sleep, do better in school, behave better, and are less likely to be obese when parents limit the amount of time spent in front of the TV and computer.

> "My two teenagers aren't allowed to post anything with their faces or personal information," says Janet. "They've asked me if they can post pictures of their dogs, and that's okay, but it stops there."

Two worthwhile rules: No phones at the dinner table, and no screens in children's bedrooms. You can explain that you're setting limits for their safety and health, and this is not debatable.

If you truly can't get your kids to hand you their phones at night, just turn off the modem at 9 p.m.

4. Collaborate With Other Parents and Teachers

Peer pressure can be irresistible for adolescents, so try to find ways to reduce it. It's reasonable to expect teachers to limit cellphone use at school, and you may be surprised by how many other parents would support other ways to curb online obsessions.

5. Make Sure Your Child Has Plenty of Opportunities for Real-Life Pursuits

Asked how parents should think about their kids' internet use, the neuroscientist Michael Merzenich, a pioneer in brain plasticity, responded: "You just have to consider what they're NOT doing when they are on screens." We've said it before, but it's worth repeating. One of the best ways parents can improve their children's lives is to insist on healthy habits, like developing skills, getting regular sleep and exercise, and spending time outdoors.

Sometimes kids already understand this and are just waiting for you to confirm it.

"One day my daughter told me that she had closed off every app," says Maria. "She said: 'It was all toxic. I didn't like the vibe, the comments people were making about each other.' I give her a lot of credit for that."

6. Spend Time Together Online

This may be the ultimate buzzkill for many adolescents. But if you catch them young enough, they may still want to share to the extent that you can get a good view of their online environment. Show you care what they have found interesting or helpful, and also what may have surprised them or made them uncomfortable.

7. As a Last Resort, Use Parental Controls

We say "last resort" because so many of them don't work, are easily evaded, and are rapidly outpaced by new technologies. If you're considering trying them anyway, it suggests you may have lost the battle for your children's trust. All that said, you may want to investigate Apple's Family Sharing settings

(Family Link on Android phones), which set time limits on internet use. Common Sense Media is a great resource that regularly reviews apps and blockers. You also might look into new smartphone models such as Pinwheel, which has built-in parental controls.

8. Keep Learning and Paying Attention

Things are changing so fast that we can only help you so much at this writing. See our Resources section for help in keeping up to date. It's time-consuming, we know, but you need to know where your child is going online.

Chapter Seven

Surviving School

W hile coping with your child's depression, you'll need to pay extra-close attention to what's going on at school. It's a critically important environment at a key time in your child's life, with constant and powerful potential impacts on mental health.

"High school," says one internet meme, "is where self-esteem, innocence and dreams go to die."

Of course, not every student suffers in high school. Many kids feel encouraged and supported by teachers and fellow students. Yet when Challenge Success, a nonprofit organization affiliated with Stanford University, surveyed more than 250,000 adolescent students nationwide, its findings were distressing:

- 95% said they were sleep-deprived.
- 77% reported stress-related health symptoms.
- 63% said they worried constantly about academics.

Teachers and students say these statistics only begin to describe the problem.

"It's pretty alarming," says Brian, a 24-year veteran teacher at a California public high school. "They're anxious about whether they'll ever get jobs. They're anxious about climate change—many of them say they can't imagine having children of their own. I've known kids who have attempted suicide. It has definitely never been this acute."

These problems were building up before the pandemic raised the stress levels of teachers, students, administration, and parents.

"What's so frustrating for me is that with us wearing masks all day, kids can't see your face, can't read the emotions, so I'm having tons of miscommunication issues," says Brian. "The best way I can connect with kids to support them academically is to get to know them, so I strive to form those relationships. But the pandemic has thrown all that to the wind."

Heightened stress can be especially hard on people struggling with mental illness. If your child is depressed, any one of several coming-of-age clichés—the nasty teacher, the mean girls, the shattered romance, or even the trigonometry quiz—can trigger a downward spiral.

Fortunately, there's a lot that you can do. This chapter will describe some of the major stumbling blocks in middle school and high school—from other students' cruelty to your child's own academic and behavioral obstacles—and offer some strategies to cope.

Bullies, Isolation, and Boycotts

Common Cruelty

You don't need to reread *Lord of the Flies* to know how cruel kids can be to each other—and especially to those who seem different. Studies show that more than a third of students with behavioral and emotional disorders face high levels of bullying. The numbers are even higher for LGBTQ+ kids—and the impacts should never be minimized.

> "School can rob your kid of potential," says Maria. "Lourdes has above-average IQ, yet at the height of her anxiety combined with the bullying at school she really believed she was 'dumb.'"

Bullying at school is unfortunately widespread. One out of every five students reports that they've been victims. The behavior can range from being teased and/or gossiped about to being excluded or physically attacked: pushed, hit, or spit at. Less than half of bullies' victims ever report it to an adult.

The harassment can occur almost anywhere—in school hallways and stairwells, inside classrooms, in the cafeteria, and on buses—but more and more, it's happening in cyberspace. In one study, one in five tweens (9–12 years old) said they'd been bullied online, bullied others online, or witnessed cyberbullying.

Your child may not tell you he or she is being bullied. Here are some ways that communicate without words:

- Unexplained cuts or bruises
- Sudden requests to stay home from school or reports of missed classes
- New complaints of headaches, stomachaches, or trouble sleeping

- Sudden disinterest in spending time with friends
- "Lost" or damaged clothes or other belongings, or new unexplained requests for more money
- Unexplained loss of appetite

If you have a vulnerable child and are lucky enough to have a choice of schools, make sure to ask if a school you're considering has an anti-bullying program. Not all schools have them, and not all programs are effective, but some research suggests that they can reduce bullying by up to 25%. At the very least you want to know that school personnel are aware of the potential problem and doing something about it. Ask how they've handed such incidents in the past, and if they have a "bystander" policy, in which other students are encouraged to befriend bullies' victims and report any bullying they see. Keep in mind that researchers have found that even merely witnessing bullying can be damaging to students' mental health.

If you suspect your child is being victimized:

- *Check in on a regular basis.* By now we hope you know how important it is to have good communication with your child. Regular chats are your best guarantee of knowing if problems are brewing outside home.
- *Encourage your child to speak up.* Getting adults involved is the only effective way to stop bullying. Urge your child to tell you or report to adults not only if he or she is the victim, but if others are also suffering.
- *Identify one adult ally.* Make sure that before each school year gets underway, you and your child have identified one empathetic adult at the school, whether it's a teacher or counselor, whom you know will be responsive to reports of bullying.
- *Don't DIY.* Tempting as it may be, don't try to fix things by contacting the bully or the bully's family. Deal with

the school. Similarly, don't put the burden of fixing the problem on your kid. Studies show that fighting back or even walking away rarely works and often makes things worse.

Friendlessness

It takes a lot of psychic energy to make and maintain friendships. Unfortunately, this may be just what your depressed child lacks right now. Being depressed can also cause a child to be irritable and push people away, leading to painful isolation.

At the start of the year or when changing schools, check into how your child's school is handling this common problem. If they don't have a plan, you might suggest they connect with Beyond Differences, a national nonprofit that identified social isolation as a problem many years before the pandemic and has come up with well-reviewed programs to combat it. The group offers a social and emotional learning curriculum, starting in middle school, that helps kids develop better relationship skills.

Your child's teacher may recommend that your child attend a school-based social-skills group. Make sure to find out what that would entail, including the credentials of whoever is leading it, and ask your child's clinician if it makes sense. Some programs may be beneficial, but they aren't right for every child, and sometimes the sheer stigma of being pulled out of class and publicly identified as socially awkward should be a deal-breaker.

When Your Child Just Says No

Many depressed children have such a difficult time at school that they end up refusing to go.

"My daughter is refusing to go to school one to two days out of every week," says Liz. "She has told me that sometimes she feels so stressed there that it's like a knife stabbing her in the back all day. Every morning she has physical symptoms, which sometimes she can overcome and sometimes not. And of course the more school she misses, the more overwhelmed and stressed she gets and it spirals into a nice tornado. We're still trying to figure out what to do about this."

As children's mental health problems have grown more prevalent, so has "school refusal." In recent years, up to 5% of students have been balking in the morning or ducking out, AWOL, later in the day, according to studies published at this writing. But school refusal is yet another problem that COVID-19 has recently made worse. Many shy students got used to attending in their jammies. Once the lockdowns ended, they resisted going back to an environment they found stressful.

"School refusal" isn't a diagnosis, but the *DSM-5* includes it as a symptom of various disorders, including major depression and posttraumatic stress disorder. This is more than a request for a "mental health day." Quite often a child is sending a distress signal. Unfortunately, the longer it goes on, the harder it is to return to the classroom.

This behavior can easily throw family life into chaos, especially when one or two parents need to leave the house on time for work and can't afford to stay home to supervise a rebellious or potentially self-harming child. Raising the stress levels for all concerned is that some schools will report parents to Child Protective Services for abetting truancy.

How should a parent respond if a 15-year-old who may already weigh more than his mother or father refuses to get out of bed? What do you do if you've watched your child have a genuine panic attack, with shortness of breath, at the thought of going to class? Some parents end up in exhausting cycles of bribery and threats. Quite a few, in desperation, have even called police to escort kids to school—although we don't recommend this outside of a genuine emergency.

School refusal can sneak up on parents. It may start with a stomachache one day and ramp up slowly to the point where your child wants to stay home every day. Pay close attention and do your best to figure out the reasons. Often the problem is social—your child is being bullied or ostracized. Or maybe there's a learning issue you haven't yet identified. Frequently, a student who can't keep up with peers falls behind to the point of losing hope of ever catching up.

Whatever the reason, a parent in most cases should resist setting a precedent for kids to avoid school, advises Southard, the wellness center coordinator. "What starts as a loving intention can be a habit that's hard to break," she says. "You want to be nurturing but you're digging a deeper ditch, and I've seen a lot of kids spiral down from there. The only way to move through anxiety is to move through the stressor, not avoid it."

Ideally your child has a therapist by now with whom you can address this problem. If not, this is a clear sign you need one. Sometimes the school psychologist, if your school is fortunate enough to have one, can help. The prescribed treatment may be for the student to attend just one class to start with, gradually increasing the exposure to the stressor (in this case school), as you would do with someone experiencing a high level of anxiety in other situations, until he or she is more comfortable staying all day. If working with the school and outpatient treatment fails to improve the situation, you may need to consider a change of environment, an option we describe below. In the most serious cases, it may be wise to consider a partial-hospitalization program.

Ruby Walker dropped out of high school for good after faking illness and then simply refusing to go. She remembers being so miserable that she kept records of her crying jags throughout the school day. "For me personally, getting out of high school was the best thing I ever did," she says today. She believes her then-undiagnosed attention-deficit/hyperactivity disorder (ADHD) contributed to her difficulties but adds: "A lot of people have a bad time in high school. I'm a mentally healthy person now but if someone said go back to high school, I'd say 'Ew, no!' Sit in class for eight hours under fluorescent lights with 30 minutes for lunch and you have to ask permission to pee? No thanks!" Ruby regained her bearings after a semester of homeschooling followed by community college. There, she could take classes that interested her, plus she could take frequent breaks from class to go outside and do jumping jacks to manage her ADHD.

Not Making the Grade?

There's no correlation between severe depression and intelligence. It's well-known that geniuses can—and often do—suffer from mental illness. Yet depression can easily prevent a student from succeeding or even staying in school, by thwarting the capacity to focus and follow rules.

Depressed children may lack the motivation and energy to do their best. New medications may cause side-effects that confound learning. Kids may also fall behind due to time spent away for hospital stays.

Three Choices for Serious Problems

If for whatever reason your son or daughter is failing at school, academically or behaviorally, your first step should be to consult with the clinician. You may need to review the treatment plan, adjusting the medication and possibly increasing or adding psychotherapy. If that doesn't work, you essentially have three choices: change the school, homeschool, or work with what you've got.

Change Schools

Sometimes there's just no fixing the environment, and you'll have to look for something different.

> "I moved my daughter to private school because her public school just couldn't meet the needs of kids like her, even with accommodations," says Janet. "The big classes were so overwhelming for her that she got in the habit of sitting in the back of the classroom, and just got lost."

Warning: Changing schools may take a lot of time and energy you may not reasonably have. If you're looking at private schools, it can also be unaffordable, unless you can get the child's original school to pay—an option we'll discuss below.

You may also end up simply trading one set of problems for another.

> "We changed school literally every year in high school," says Charlene. "At each one there was a different set of problems that would emerge after a few weeks or months. But mostly the story was the same: She couldn't make friends and couldn't keep up with the work, and she got more and more depressed."

Still, the evidence from research is what you might expect. Several studies suggest that adolescents attending schools with better social climates experience less depression, drug use, and bullying. How do you find these islands of quality? Start with the counselor at your child's school, but you may also want to contract with a private educational counselor, whose job it is to know how to find the right fit. They aren't cheap, but the right one can make a big difference.

Homeschool

Let's acknowledge right away that homeschooling a child with severe depression is *not* for the faint of heart. It may also require one parent to stay home to supervise, which can lead to resentment if you're not careful. Depressed kids can sometimes be so irritable that it's a big ask for a parent to give up those hours of freedom. And of course it's not just time that's required: Giving your child a good or even adequate experience will take a lot of research, networking with like-minded friends and maybe homeschooling consultants, and planning activities with other kids so your child isn't totally isolated. Are you honestly ready to take on these challenges? If so, the bright side is you'll be joining a trend that was well underway before the pandemic and has been growing even faster ever since. At this writing, roughly 5 million US students are going to school at home.

COVID-19 has given parents the world over a crash course in modified homeschooling, and many found it a good alternative to the social pressures and conformity of regular school. By October 2020, the US Census Bureau reported that 11% of US households were homeschooling—more than double the rate at the start of the pandemic. (This was genuine homeschooling, not simply remote learning.)

For Black and other minority families, the growth has been considerably sharper. Whereas roughly 3% of Black students were homeschooled before the pandemic, that number had risen to 16% by the end of 2020. Many parents have told researchers that they made the choice to protect their kids from the racism and lower expectations in public schools.

While the quality of homeschooling varies from home to home, at least some homeschooled students perform just as well or better academically as their peers. Kids who vary from the norm—especially those with concentration problems that make it hard to sit still—may in fact thrive from being free of the negative feedback and social pressures while also able to explore and develop their own interests.

Work With What You've Got

Most parents—meaning those who can't find a public school nirvana or afford to pay private school tuition or quit their day jobs to homeschool—will need to work with their kids' current school. The silver lining to this is that once you've learned the system you may find that public schools offer all sorts of support that your child can't get anywhere else. Under federal law, public schools must provide a "free and appropriate public education" to all students, including those with mental and physical disabilities. That's true regardless of your income level. Still, there's a lot a parent can do to help make their kids' experience more than simply appropriate. Before we describe the applicable laws, we'd like to offer some high-level suggestions.

Winning Strategies for Wherever You Are

Forge Alliances

During these crucial years, consider yourself the ambassa-dor and even sometimes translator for a child who may be all too easily misunderstood. That means making friends, or at least alliances, with other parents, teachers, and school administrators. Even if you're holding down a job (or two) and raising other kids, try to find time to reach out.

Enlist Your Peers

Other parents of children with mental health issues will often be your best resources at school. Some will have already figured out solutions to problems you're facing and can steer you to the most sympathetic teachers, clinicians, and programs. Not least, other parents who know what you're going through can serve as stress-relieving antidotes to all those other parents who're so much quicker to judge, gossip, and ostracize.

> "My son was a wrestler," says one mother. "Before he went into the hospital, I'd go to his practices, and all the parents would talk to me. After he got out of the hospital and went back to wrestling, there was suddenly nobody to talk to. They all went to sit on the other side of the room. I think they just didn't know what to say."

It's easy to find online forums for parents of children with specific disorders. But since real-life friendships can be so much more fulfilling, here are some ways to forge them:

- Look for a special education parent–teacher association (PTA)—known as SEPTAs—in your district.
- If your district lacks a SEPTA, find tips for launching one on the national PTA website.
- Ask school administrators if they might confidentially contact other parents in your boat for an initial coffee meeting to see if you click.
- Look for a local chapter of the Depression and Bipolar Support Alliance (DBSA), further details of which are in our Resources section.

Sometimes groups that began as coffee klatches morph into powerful lobbyists for school-wide and local change.

> "It's amazing how many people you meet when you are open about this issue—how many people will say, my child was just diagnosed, or my nephew or my neighbor," says one mother who became a local education activist. She began by joining a local support group and eventually created her own. "Unless somebody starts the conversation," she says, "everyone walks around not talking."

Polish Apples

Connecting with teachers is one of the best ways you can improve your child's daily life at school. We understand this may be hard. In grade school, teachers and your kid wanted you on campus, and volunteering may have been a breeze. Now your child has many different teachers and may be embarrassed by seeing you anywhere in public.

You're going to have to be more tactful and subtle than you were in those early years. Don't do your hobnobbing in front of your child. But seize whatever opportunities you can.

> "At the open house at the beginning of the year, I go up to the teachers and shake their hands," says one mother. "I look them right in the eye, and I hold their hand so they remember my face. I say, 'Hi, I'm Roberta Smith. I'm Jake's mom.' And then I say, 'Listen, if you have any problems, can you call me right away? Because we can chat about these things.' I make myself very approachable, and they call me."

Don't forget to also reach out to the school counselor or psychologist, assuming the school has one or both. This contact may end up being more important than the teachers, especially if there's a problem.

After the initial meeting, stay in touch throughout the year. And don't just email. Write a note or call. Teachers are busy, but you may be surprised by their willingness to communicate, if you reach out with skill and compassion.

"More and more, parents just aren't talking to teachers," says Brian. "We've moved everything online, so if anything, they'll email. But some never reach out. In the past, maybe 30 parents out of 120 kids would contact me directly. These days it's down to four! But the more a parent communicates with the teachers and gets to know them, the more the teacher can help that kid."

Don't forget to let teachers know when things are going *right*. An occasional thank-you note or small gift, like fruit or cookies, can go a long way. Some parents have won teachers' hearts by writing an appreciative letter to the principal. If you have the time, you might try to establish yourself as an asset to the school by participating in fundraising efforts or volunteering in the office. All of this is a down payment for the time when you'll need to ask for support.

Manage Your Fear

It's now time for a note about emotions—starting with yours. We absolutely get that you may be stressed out, exhausted, panicked, and angry. Your human instinct is to do all you can to protect your child, and if you suspect your child is being mistreated by adults or other kids, you may quite understandably arrive at school in a fury. You'll need to control that urge, however, if you truly wish to help your child. No one responds well to anger, blame, or threats.

Pick a time when both you and the teacher are reasonably relaxed—and make an appointment; don't just drop by. It may also help you to bring notes of the points you want to get across.

Then, pay attention to the way you communicate. Use those classic "I statements" rather than "you statements"; that is, "I noticed Johnny staying up all night trying to finish his project," rather than "You're giving the kids too much homework." To convey respect, try "reflective listening," in which you subtly echo what the other person says so that he or she knows you care and are paying attention. You can say something like "I'm hearing you say that Johnny has been distracting the class." Or even, "It sounds like you've got a lot to manage." Don't waste time talking about all the problems your Johnny has had in the past; focus on the issue at hand.

If you're sending an email, read it aloud before pushing "send." At times when your emotions are running high, it may even help to send it first to a sympathetic friend, since in the heat of the moment it may be hard for you to catch yourself being subtly or not-so-subtly aggressive.

> "The other day I looked back on all my emails to Matt's sixth-grade teacher during a single week, and it was really embarrassing," says Beth. "I somehow lost track of just how many I was sending and how furious they sounded. I'm not sure I can blame her for not answering after the first three."

Try giving the teacher the benefit of the doubt. Most want to do a good job for every student yet were under unusual stress long before the pandemic played havoc with their lives, and in most cases must manage scores of students a day. If your child is acting out or sloughing off, even if it's due to illness or medication side-effects, you can't expect 100% tolerance—especially if the teachers don't understand what's going on. You'll get the best results if you arrive with an attitude that says, "We're all in this together."

If you learn that a teacher is being unreasonably intolerant with your child, it's perfectly appropriate for you to express your concerns to the teacher or the principal. Once again, try to avoid sounding accusatory. Instead, project an attitude that you're on the same team. That may be all it takes to enlist the teacher's cooperation. But if all else fails, insist on a change. Some teachers are exceptionally skilled at dealing with "difficult" kids and can make a huge difference in your child's attitude about school. But others lack the wherewithal and may even do serious damage to a vulnerable child.

When you do find an understanding teacher, be open about your child's challenges and strengths. Share all the relevant information, including about medication, to the extent your child is comfortable with that, and show the teacher you're willing to hear suggestions about the best way to work together.

Know Your Rights

It may seem like ancient history today, but until 1975, millions of US kids with disabilities—from being deaf or blind to having serious behavioral problems—couldn't attend public schools. (A child who used a wheelchair was considered a fire hazard!) Those who did go to school did so at institutions far from home, at their parents' expense, and in many cases were simply warehoused.

This was all before two landmark lawsuits on behalf of excluded children, which helped lead to two sweeping federal laws. The first, in 1973, was Section 504 of the Rehabilitation Act, a civil rights law prohibiting schools receiving federal funding from discriminating against students with disabilities. Two years later, the Education for All Handicapped Children Act—later renamed the Individuals with Disabilities Education Act (IDEA)—provided funding to remove barriers to mainstream education and give qualified students an individualized education program (IEP).

We'll elaborate on each of these laws below, and there's a chart in the Appendix that lays out the main differences. In a nutshell: 504 accommodations are significantly more informal and assume less involvement by parents.

Under the IDEA, schools must involve parents in every step of the process, whereas a 504 plan simply requires schools to notify parents if they decide to evaluate a student to determine if he or she qualifies for special consideration.

The rules for 504 plans vary across school districts, which determine who may qualify for accommodations. Often the plan doesn't even need to be in writing, as is required under IDEA.

A 504 plan may work just fine for students whose symptoms are mild to moderate, yet keep in mind that your child may need more help than it can provide.

"Schools love to provide accommodations because they don't cost anything," says Howey. "But accommodations should never substitute for special education, which is specialized instruction designed to meet the unique needs of an individual child."

Schools may prefer to route your child into a 504 plan because unlike IDEA provisions, it doesn't cost money. But some parents have found this path to be frustrating, in part because schools are often less inclined to take 504 accommodations seriously.

If you're requesting any sort of special help for your child, we have three specific recommendations: Find a lawyer—at least for an initial consultation. Put all serious requests in writing. And keep records of all relevant documents.

Find a Lawyer

For any serious conflict with your child's school, it's worthwhile to consult with a special-education attorney. Many won't charge for an initial meeting. Find one in your area or state in the directory for the Council of Parent Attorneys and Advocates (COPAA.org). If your state lacks attorneys with this specialization, you may want to look in a neighboring state. Use caution if you choose to hire an advocate, however; some are quite good, but they aren't held to formal standards. Ask for references or find other ways to get a sense of the track record.

Write It Down

> "I remember my 15-year-old granddaughter and I were having a discussion about bullying," says Howey. "She had witnessed someone being bullied and said she went to the school counselor, and nothing happened, so she'd never do that again. I said: 'That's because you didn't put it in writing. It didn't happen if it isn't in writing.'"

Thanks, Granma, right? This may be a lot to expect from a teenager. But Howey has a good point for you, personally, to keep in mind. Say your child has been bullied and tells you about it. The natural thing for you to do is call the teacher or principal. And maybe something will get done. But there is something about a letter. It adds a sense of conferring responsibility a phone call simply can't match.

In particular, we want you to know about a kind of notification known as a "Gebser letter," a sample of which we provide in the Appendix. "Gebser" refers to a 1998 Supreme Court case that wasn't about special education or bullying—it dealt with a suit by the mother of a high school student who was having an affair with a teacher. But through the years, it has become a way to refer to a letter that puts a school on notice that bullying—or any other sort of discrimination or wrong treatment of a student with special needs—has occurred. School administrators pay attention to these kinds of letters, because the implication is that they've been put on notice and are responsible to see that the behavior stops—or possibly risk a lawsuit.

As a general rule, it's also a good idea to keep notes of telephone conversations with teachers and school leaders, which leads us to our third main suggestion.

Keep Records

As soon as you know you'll be requesting special help from your child's school, start keeping track of all relevant documents and notes. Consider maintaining a binder to keep copies of the following:

- Medical documents, including those relating to symptoms of your child's disorder and any side-effects of your child's medications
- Progress reports or report cards
- Results of standardized or proficiency tests
- Any formal letters and notices, informal notes, and e-mails from medical providers, teachers, and other school staff
- Notes on verbal communications, including phone conversations and face-to-face meetings
- Representative samples of schoolwork
- Financial records, including invoices and receipts, for services you pay for privately to advance your child's education

Make a list of the documents and arrange them in chronological order.

504 Accommodations: School Services "Lite"

If your child isn't too impaired to handle the normal challenges of public school, with a few exceptions, you may want to ask for help under Section 504. It's easier for students to qualify, since it merely requires that they have a physical or mental impairment that substantially limits one or more major life activities—a standard that any student with major depression is likely to meet. Many parents seek 504 modifications while waiting to see if their child qualifies for IDEA support.

This may be all-around a quicker, easier process than the one provided under the IDEA. Work with your child's mental health provider to see if the supports offered are adequate, or if you need to move up to the next level. Remember, a 504 plan guarantees merely a "free, appropriate public education" for students with disabilities—meaning an education comparable to students without disabilities, but not one designed to meet the student's unique needs.

The student may receive easy-to-manage supports such as sitting in front of the class, being allowed extra time to complete tests, and getting a break on homework or classwork. You might also enlist a teacher or counselor to help your child take medication—just be careful how you do this, to reduce the risk of shaming.

If you've chosen this route, start by sending a written request to the school. (Remember, avoid the phone if possible and put things in writing!) You don't need a formal evaluation, but any medical records supporting your child's diagnosis may help. You may also want to ask your child's clinician to write a letter explaining how your child's disability limits his or her functioning. Once the 504 coordinator receives your request, the school may invite you to meet with a team of teachers and staff to see if your child is eligible and, if so, review a proposed plan. Most schools do this, although there's no formal requirement. Note that even as these federal laws exist, states have sometimes dramatically different ways of interpreting them, so you can't assume practices will be the same throughout the country.

IDEA: The Heftier Choice

If 504 assistance isn't enough, you can request special services paid for under the IDEA and provided for your child through an IEP. IEPs cover students meeting the criteria for one or more of more than a dozen categories of disabilities, including being deaf, blind, or autistic, or having brain injuries or disabling orthopedic problems.

The IDEA categories relevant to depression are "emotional disturbance" and a catch-all known as "other health impairment." You may prefer to seek a classification of "other health impairment," which doesn't carry the stigma of labeling someone as emotionally disturbed.

"EMOTIONAL DISTURBANCE"

To qualify for an "emotional disturbance" under the IDEA, a student must have at least one of the following problems "over a long period of time and to a marked degree that adversely affects educational performance":

- An inability to learn that cannot be explained by intellectual, sensory, or health factors

- An inability to build or maintain satisfactory interpersonal relationships with peers and teachers
- Inappropriate types of behavior or feelings under normal circumstances
- A general pervasive mood of unhappiness or depression
- A tendency to develop physical symptoms or fears associated with personal or school problems

("Emotional disturbance" also includes schizophrenia.)

"OTHER HEALTH IMPAIRMENT"

In contrast to "emotional disturbance," "other health impairment" doesn't specifically mention depression, but the criteria will easily apply:

1. The student has limited strength or vitality or altered alertness, which results in limited alertness with respect to the educational environment.
2. The cause is a chronic or acute health problem, such as ADHD, asthma, diabetes, epilepsy, a heart condition, hemophilia, lead poisoning, leukemia, nephritis, rheumatic fever, or sickle cell anemia.
3. The student's educational performance is adversely affected.

THE EVALUATION

If you're seeking help under IDEA, your child has the right to a free evaluation of his or her learning impediments, paid for by the school. Either you or the school may request this. If you initiate the request, be sure to put it in writing. It's best to send the letter by certified mail or get a receipt when you hand-deliver it. Be specific about what you see as problems, but don't ask for a specific test or diagnosis. Maybe your fifth grader is still counting on his fingers. Or your daughter has turned in only 6 of 30 homework assignments that year.

Once you've made your request, the school must either complete a full evaluation or notify you in writing of the refusal and the reasons for it and advise you of your rights. If your child has been refused, ask to meet with school officials to make sure you understand the reasons and the appeal process.

You may want to get your own evaluation even if the school is willing to do one. The law says the school evaluator(s) should be "a multi-disciplinary team" with "trained and knowledgeable" personnel who use "technically sound instruments," but this is sometimes more aspirational than real. If you can show that the school ignored the concerns in your letter or is unable to do an adequate evaluation, you may be able to get it to pay. Also check if your insurance will reimburse you. Most won't, but Medicaid may.

Assuming the school agrees to evaluate your child, you must give your consent in writing and the evaluation must take place within 60 days, unless the law in your state says otherwise. The evaluation should determine whether your child qualifies as disabled and what his or her educational needs must be.

Note that this can be a drawn-out process. If you feel like the clock is ticking and your child is losing valuable time, consider writing a letter requesting that the school expedite the evaluation.

The Individualized Education Program

Once evaluation results are available, your school must invite you to an eligibility meeting where you and the other members of your child's team will decide whether your child is eligible for special education and related services. Consider asking your child's doctor or therapist to attend this meeting, perhaps by teleconferencing to save on travel time (and costs).

If your child is eligible, your school must develop an IEP within 30 days and must invite you to a meeting to help write it. The resulting written statement must include, at minimum:

- An assessment of your child's level of functioning
- A description of the special education and related services to be provided—including *where* the services will be provided, if the school can't offer them
- A statement of academic and functional goals to be assessed each year
- A description of how progress will be measured

It must then be reviewed at least once a year and revised as needed.

If you don't agree with the plan, state this at the meeting, write down that you do not agree, and give your note of disagreement to whomever is in charge of the meeting. As with all documents, sign and date it and keep a copy in your files.

Consider requesting another meeting to try to work out a compromise. In some states, you can ask for a meeting chaired by a neutral party, or for mediation. Before choosing either of these routes, consider talking to an experienced attorney.

The IEP may list relatively minor strategies, such as more time on tests, or being able to sit in the front row, but also may determine that your child needs intensive care at a setting outside the school. The guiding principle is that a student should be placed in the "least restrictive" environment. Your child shouldn't be sent to a separate special education class if his or her needs can be met in a regular classroom. But if your child needs round-the-clock residential care, the school may be required to pay at least for part of that expense.

IEPs take time and energy, but they do more than help prepare a student for "further education, employment, and independent living," as is the law's mission. They've also saved many parents a considerable amount of money.

As we've noted earlier, your child may qualify for some psychological services, including school-based counseling, under this law. Another possibility is that the school might pay for placement in a therapeutic day program or even a long-term residential facility. These more extreme measures usually require a due process hearing or sometimes also an appeal to a state or federal court. Don't expect immediate relief.

THE FUNCTIONAL BEHAVIORAL ASSESSMENT

If your child's depression is causing disciplinary problems, you need to know about the functional behavioral assessment (FBA), which is part of the IDEA law. This could be part of the IDEA evaluation, but any parent may request one if there's reason to believe a student is misbehaving because of mental illness. Asking for an FBA in writing as soon as you recognize the risk is also a strategic tactic to reduce the chance that your child will be punished, suspended, or expelled because of behavior beyond his or her control.

The assessment should be led by someone trained in understanding behavior, and it should look at where and when misbehavior is occurring.

"I used to do my best to get kicked out of math class, because I have dyscalculia, and knew it was more socially acceptable to be a troublemaker than be branded 'stu-pid,'" says Howey.

An Array of Supports

Regardless of IEPs or 504s, teachers should still expect students to make their best efforts each day. The supports should be designed only to help them make the most of their capabilities.

The accommodations aim to address two main groups of problems that can interfere with academic success: stress and poor communication. Stress relief is especially important, given that stress at school can destabilize a student who is emotionally fragile. Kids with common coexisting issues, such as ADHD and anxiety, may need more time with tests and assignments. As you develop a list of accommodations, ask your child for his or her input, which if nothing else may help get initial buy-in. Ideally, however, your child should take ownership of his or her plan over time, honing those important self-advocacy skills.

Following are some common accommodations that might fit into either a 504 plan or an IEP.

RELIEVING STRESS
Scheduling

- Allow for a later start or a shorter day, to improve sleep and reduce stress.
- Schedule the most stimulating classes early in the day to get the student interested.
- Schedule the hardest classes for the time of day when the student is usually most alert.

"I arrange it so my son never has two classes in a row where he has to sit still," says one parent. For instance, her son might follow a math class with physical education.

Classroom Activities

- Provide movement breaks at regular intervals.
- Allow a water bottle at the desk.
- Permit frequent bathroom breaks and self-imposed "time-outs" if the student is feeling overwhelmed.
- Use alternative discipline tactics for behavior problems. Traditional approaches to discipline don't work well when kids have depression. Some alternatives could include giving a student more time to comply with a request or writing up a list of options from which a student may choose.

Testing

- Break long tests into smaller segments.
- Simplify test instructions.
- Allow extra time for tests.
- Provide a test room away from other students and distractions.
- Offer other assignments as an alternative to high-stress tests.

One mother, whose son was in a drug rehabilitation program for two hours a day, three days a week, persuaded his school to give him high school credit for attending, arguing that this experience would help him more in life than any history class or English class.

Homework

- Simplify homework instructions.
- Extend deadlines for projects.

Improving Communication

- Have the student meet with a teacher on arriving at school each day to gauge his or her ability to succeed in certain classes. Potentially provide alternatives to stressful activities on difficult days.
- Conduct regular and frequent meetings or phone calls between teachers and parents about the student's classroom performance.

Be a Squeaky Wheel

Don't make the mistake of assuming that once an IEP is in place, you can check out. Many parents say they've had to bird-dog schools to make sure they're following the law, implementing a plan that's working well for their child.

At the same time, know that your child's teacher may be overwhelmed with the increasing numbers of students whose families are demanding accommodations.

"Ten years ago, maybe 10% of my students had an IEP or 504 plan," says Brian. "Now it's 30 to 40%. In many cases, they do need support, but in some cases you'll have these savvy parents who are simply trying to get their child an edge. The result is I've got 30 to 40 reports I have to read, all with different sorts of accommodations. Honestly, I don't read them. I don't have that kind of time. I try instead to get to know the kid."

Brian has a smart tip for kids and parents coping with mood disorders in school.

> "When I reflect on the students who've had the most success despite their challenges, it's really been those who've had a clear sense of their disorder—without denying it—and could talk about it with me," he says. "I'm thinking in particular of one girl who would occasionally get triggered by something and then fly out of the room wailing in emotional agony, but who would then return later in the day and apologize, and talk about it, without shame or frustration. She was also an incredible student, so maybe was special in that way, but her ability to establish that clear, trusting dialogue was key to her being so successful."

COVID-19 Chaos

The pandemic has had a particularly disruptive impact on students receiving special services. In many cases, schools that shut down simply suspended provisions of IEPs. In several states, parents filed lawsuits complaining that their children had been unfairly harmed. In early 2020, US Education Secretary Betsy DeVos said students who missed out should be re-evaluated on return to school and receive "compensatory services." At this writing, schools were still struggling to catch up.

We recommend that you avoid getting mired in legal conflicts if possible. But do keep insisting on high-quality support—whether or not your school is physically open.

Chapter Eight

Life After High School

S o your son or daughter has safely reached age 18.

In the past few years, you've done a great job tracking down effective clinicians, finding ways to afford them, keeping stress down at home, and working diligently with the schools. Your child may still be struggling but feels ready to launch— and you cautiously agree.

Now there's one more major task on your plate in this last year of adolescence.

It's time to help prepare your child for life outside the nest.

Make a Plan

You may be justifiably anxious about this next step. Both you and your teen may be feeling overwhelmed by the choices ahead. Transitions can be stressful for anyone, especially when they're as big as graduating school and possibly moving away from home. Yet as always, learning about your options may help calm you down. You and your child can create a plan to help both of you sleep better at night. Happily, it's by now more likely that your son or daughter has matured to the point that you'll now have a genuine partner in this project.

Remember—and remind your child—that taking a job or signing a lease is not an irrevocable step. For any Plan A, make a Plan B. Focus on keeping the stress as low as possible. If your child is moving out, be clear that he or she has a safe base with you and can return home if needed.

Manage Expectations

Now's a good time for you to listen more than talk, and to restrain any impulse to push. When you do offer your opinion, you'll want to walk the line between optimism and realism. Be mindful of the messages you've sent in the past. Even without saying it, your teen may feel he or she has let you down by not enrolling in your alma mater. Find a noncondescending way to communicate that you're proud your child has graduated—and is going to community college, or taking a creative gap year, or finding a job, or whatever else is in the works. There will be time for course corrections, if needed. Right now, you need a plan for the next year.

Lay the Foundation

Assuming your son or daughter is moving out, this is a good time to go over some fundamentals: reminders of all you've both learned about self-management and care. Consider relaying the suggestions below in a few, spaced-out heart-to-hearts, instead of a single, scary data dump.

Talk about the importance of adequate sleep, good nutrition, regular exercise, and avoiding impulsive behavior, including drugs, alcohol, and ill-advised hookups. Review the value of reliable routines and regular check-ins with parents. In our age of increasingly remote work and school, stress the value of real-life close friends, seen regularly, in person.

Impress on your child, if you haven't already done so enough, the importance of staying on any needed medication. And make a plan together in the event of a mental health emergency away from home. This could include a rule that you're allowed to call a friend of theirs if you haven't heard from them as expected.

If you haven't already done so, now is also a good time to talk about managing money responsibly, much as you would with any other teenager, but with some gentle extra emphasis on curbing impulsivity. Sometimes bouts of depression can lead to poor choices, such as unaffordable shopping binges. Consider setting up a credit card with a low limit to start out, with the condition that you, your partner, or another trusted adult monitor the spending.

Is College in the Cards?

Consider With Care

Even if your teen is set on college, you'll need to proceed carefully. Higher education isn't the best choice for everyone, especially for someone who is emotionally fragile and straight out of high school. The writing has been on the wall about this for several years; a recent study found that nearly 40% of students who enroll in four-year colleges still don't have a degree six years later. Many of them return home, lost, discouraged, and even traumatized.

If your teen is still struggling emotionally, give serious thought to alternatives, even if it means letting go of a dream.

If you believe your child is ready for more independence and challenge, you should still set some limits. By no means send your kid to school across the country if he or she has no experience living alone.

Your child may fare best by living at home and attending a community college for the first year or two. If that works out well, you might both feel more confident to move on to the bigger challenge, which could include a four-year school farther from home.

Fill the Gap

Taking a "gap year" has been an increasingly popular option in recent years. Whether you sign up for a formal program, which can be expensive, or design one of your own, the trick is to make sure you're not wasting time and money. It will take some thought and research to decide on a good use of the year. The plan could include volunteering, working as an intern, or taking a low-skill job to save up money. Talk to your child's high school counselor and carefully vet programs. The Gap Year Association offers accreditation and its website is a good early guide to programs, costs, and financial aid. Check out the array of enviable choices, including learning Mandarin in Taipei, conversing with national intellectual leaders at the School of the *New York Times*, mastering white-water rafting in the American Southwest, or interning with community organizations in Argentina. Internships are a particularly wise choice for students with or without specific emotional challenges. It's always a good idea to investigate what a job entails before deciding on a career.

When choosing a program, pay special attention to the structure it provides, since that can be a helpful guard against anxiety and depression.

You may want to consider a "gap" program specifically designed to prepare students for adult life. Since 2014, hundreds of students with mental disabilities have graduated from NITEO, at Boston College, a six-month program aimed at helping kids develop the skills and resilience to go on to higher education or a job. NITEO is a small program trying to fill a big need, but similar efforts are emerging. Fountain House, a national nonprofit, runs a 14-week college re-entry program for students aged 18 to 30 who left school due to mental illness.

Vocational training is another good option to ease the transition into the working world. Many colleges also now have co-op programs, in which students can work part-time, which helps reduce financial stress and provides structure. For low-income families, the US Job Corps provides eight months to two years of academic and career training plus housing to kids aged 16 to 24.

Investigate the Angles

If you're helping with your high school senior's college application (and what parents aren't doing that these days?) don't hesitate to seek consideration of time lost to depression, assuming your child agrees.

> "It was only after my daughter's freshman year that she tried medication," says Julie. "After that, she got all A's. So I'm writing a letter asking them to ignore the grades she got in her first year."

And when researching potential scholarships, check out the specially designated aid for children with disabilities, including mental illness, offered by organizations such as Google and Wells Fargo. Scholarships.com is a good first place to look, but you can also check with your child's high school counselor or contact the financial aid department of the college your child may attend.

College Mental Health Resources

Just as there is a significantly increased need for mental health providers throughout the country, there is also increased need for mental health services on college campuses—partly because kids who in previous generations would not have made it to college due to struggles with their mental health are now able to attend because of great advances in treatment. What this means, though, is that the use of college counseling centers is on the rise, having increased 30% between 2009 and 2015— and it continues to increase.

> "In my son's freshman year he became so depressed that he checked into the psychiatric hospital off-campus," says Beth. "I kept calling the mental health clinic and couldn't get any straight answers, so I flew across the country to get him out. When I arrived, I learned there were seven other kids in the hospital from the same school."

If your child does go away to school, it's important to know that a medical leave of absence may be necessary if a crisis occurs. There is no shame in taking a break from school in order to get healthy. As such you will want to find out what your child's school's policy and protocol is on medical leaves of absence due to mental health issues, and re-entry into the institution once they've recovered.

When considering schools with your child, ask about the ratio of therapists to students. What is the school's policy for mental health crises? How effective is its disability office? What classroom accommodations are available? Some schools are better resourced than others in this regard; some even use their "wellness" services in their marketing. Assuming things look good, encourage your child to self-advocate, seek accommodations, and make use of the disability office and other resources as needed—but only as needed, and discreetly. Not every professor or even fellow student will be sensitive to learning about another student's mental health struggles.

Go with your son or daughter to check out a couple of schools. Questions will arise on campus that might not occur at home, and it's a great way to show your teen that he or she is not alone in this decision.

Get It in Writing

Unfortunately, you cannot necessarily rely on a college to contact you in a crisis. That's why it's important for you to get your teen's written permission in advance to communicate with the school about health issues. Privacy rules are complicated, with sometimes different interpretations depending on the school. But many a parent has been surprised and dismayed by a college's refusal to share a student's health information, even in a crisis, citing HIPAA (the Health Insurance Portability and Accountability Act) or FERPA (the Family Educational Rights and Privacy Act) restrictions. That said, exceptions to confidentiality and privacy laws can be made when a student is considered a threat to self or others.

Sometimes a conscientious faculty member will reach out, and sometimes a parent can get answers even without a child's permission, by being sufficiently noisy and insistent. But you may not have the wherewithal to do that when you're panicked, so better to take simple precautions. Before your child leaves for school, call the campus information office and ask for any forms you can sign in advance.

The JED Foundation, a national mental health nonprofit group, gives this advice for parents worried about a faraway student's mental health:

1. *Call the dean.* If you're concerned after speaking to your child, you can call the dean of students, the vice president of student affairs, or the counseling office for an independent check.

2. *Report emergencies immediately.* If your child is talking about violence or self-harm or sounds markedly different from usual (such as speaking incoherently), let the counseling service or even campus security know immediately.

3. *Get help if you're having trouble separating.* If you find yourself constantly worrying, despite reassurances from your child and campus professionals, you may need to talk it out with a professional.

There is some good news. Many colleges and universities around the country are now expanding and reshaping their student mental health services. For example, the JED Foundation has developed a rapidly expanding national program, called JED Campus, which consults with institutions of higher learning on how to improve their mental health systems and supports, as well as suicide prevention programs. As of this writing, there are more than 370 JED Campuses, and recent findings by the Foundation indicate that the ability of colleges and campuses to protect the mental health of their students has improved considerably.

Joining the Workforce?

Planning the Best Fit

Whether or not you have a college-bound student, now's a good time to brainstorm about future jobs with the best chance of preserving mental health. Satisfying work can be a major source of well-being, but choosing that work can be tricky. It is best to anticipate some possible pitfalls.

Kids with severe depression should consider ways to minimize stress on the job. Working at home—which has become a lot more common—is one way, although if that's alluring, you should also talk to your child about how to avoid the significant risks of social isolation.

A regular schedule with predictable tasks is preferable to shift work with changing hours or working on projects with intense deadlines. That way it's easier to avoid dangerous disruptions in sleep and healthy routines like getting enough exercise. Part-time, flexible work may be better than a full-time job, if that's possible. The gig economy is booming, but jumping from gig to gig can be stressful.

Self-awareness is a major contributor to success at work for *anyone*, so we hope by now your child has had enough counseling and practice to recognize his or her triggers and know how to manage anxiety. Consider jobs that are flexible enough to provide breaks when needed. Copywriting, technical writing, and computer programming may be good options for kids with relevant skills. Accounting is another skilled job that can be flexible and remote. Outside the home, low-stress, structured jobs include being an office receptionist, audiologist, or sonographer. Some easily stressed kids flourish by working with animals, and thanks to the pandemic, when so many families got new pets, there has never been a bigger demand for dog walkers. Landscaping and gardening are also low-stress and flexible jobs that don't entail a lot of interpersonal conflict.

There are lots of jobs available in caregiving of all kinds, but surveys show caregivers on average are extraordinarily stressed, with a high risk for depression. On the other hand, being unemployed—and uninsured—is also a major threat to mental health.

Talk to your teen about his or her strengths and passions. Encourage him or her to visit the high school career counselor and talk it over with the therapist. Look into internships to see if a certain job makes sense. And take it as slowly as you need.

If your child is considering a specific new job, look into the mental health benefits provided, as these can vary widely. What is the insurance coverage? Are there on-site resources? Many employers now offer such benefits, and younger generations, who've been more open about talking about mental illness, have been more outspoken in requesting them.

Even so, your child should think carefully about how much private information to share with the employer, at least at first. You can't predict the reaction, so the best plan may be to research the benefits independently and wait at least a few months before requesting any of the accommodations we describe below.

Rights on the Job

Your young adult should be aware of government support for people disabled by mental illness.

The Americans with Disabilities Act (ADA) protects people from discrimination if a physical or mental impairment "substantially limits one or more major life activities."

Reasonable accommodations could include flexible working hours, an option to work remotely, health insurance with mental health care, a workplace with reduced distractions, permission to drink water during the day or take mental health breaks, or time off with or without pay. Some employers may tap their disability insurance to pay at least a partial salary during this time.

These accommodations aren't automatic: Employees need to request them. You're not required to specify a psychiatric disorder. Saying you need time off to adjust to a new medication may be enough. But you may also need to provide some written documentation.

An employer can deny any accommodations that would cause the company undue hardship—for instance, by being excessively costly for a relatively small business.

For more information, call the US Department of Justice ADA Information Line at 800-514-0301 or go to www.ada.gov.

You and your child should also be aware of the following:

The US Equal Employment Opportunity Commission considers complaints by employees who believe they've been fired or denied accommodations unfairly. Claims must be filed within 180 days of the violation.

The Family and Medical Leave Act (FMLA) allows up to 12 weeks of unpaid leave during a year. For more information, call 866-487-9243 or visit the US Department of Labor website.

Social Security Disability Insurance (SSDI) provides income for qualified employees who can't work due to a documented mental or physical disability that is either intermittent or continuous.

Mood disorders may qualify for SSDI payments, but the requirements are strict, and applications are often rejected.

Call 800-772-1213 or visit the Social Security website for more information.

Chapter Nine

Coping With Crises

O f course you're worried. Your son or daughter may have stopped talking with you, while spending hours alone behind a closed door. Maybe you're getting calls from irate teachers. Maybe you've seen signs of drug use. Most haunting is the fear that there will be no end to this, or rather too final and heartbreaking an end. Past generations of parents didn't worry this much about death by suicide, did they? Was that just because people hushed it up?

Partly, but not entirely. Remember those national statistics we've mentioned. If your child is seriously depressed, you need to be prepared for all sorts of emergencies. Until now, we've given you guidance on the day to day. This chapter is for when things fall apart.

Trigger alert: This chapter will deal with some of the scariest and hardest experiences you may have in caring for someone with serious mental illness. For many of you, it may never get this bad. But we want to arm you with the best possible information. Hope for the best, in other words, but make sure you never regret not preparing for the worst.

> "I continue to arraign and prosecute myself for every sign, every clue, I missed," writes Rep. Jamie Raskin (D-Md.), a former law professor who lost his 25-year-old son Tommy to suicide in 2020. Tommy had suffered from depression that his parents later said had been "a kind of relentless torture in the brain" that became "overwhelming and unyielding and unbearable."

Sending Out an SOS

Many adolescents challenge authority and break rules. Many will lie, turn sullen, stay out late, and keep secrets, and the majority will experiment with alcohol or drugs. Yet it's common for kids who are struggling with severe depression to go farther, sometimes becoming defiant, hostile, and aggressive. If your son or daughter is behaving this way, you may need to remind yourself that your child is not your enemy, determined to ruin your life. He or she urgently needs help.

No matter how ugly things may get, remember what we've told you about not succumbing to shame. We've spoken with parents whose children have whacked them in the face, stolen the car, or been caught selling drugs. We're not saying you have to love their behavior, but loving them, as hard as it may sometimes be, may be the one thing that gets all of you through this.

Watch for Self-Harm

Cutting, burning, and other types of self-harm are surprisingly common among adolescents at large. As many as one in five at some point will have hurt themselves on purpose in a significant way (i.e., more than picking at a cuticle) during their lifetimes. More girls than boys engage in this behavior, which is also more common in kids who've been bullied, have low-self-esteem, or know a friend who has engaged in this behavior. But the numbers rise most dramatically when an adolescent is depressed.

Inducing pain can be a way to manage emotions that are otherwise intolerable. It can also become addictive. But in most cases, it's easy for a parent to miss. For many kids, this behavior is less a cry for help than a private coping method, and it's common for them to try to hide their injuries, cutting and sometimes burning themselves on the shoulders, abdomen, or thighs in ways that can be covered by clothing. Consider it a possible warning sign if your child suddenly favors long-sleeved t-shirts or turtlenecks.

On the other hand, your child may have found friends who are also self-harming and is trading tips on techniques.

> "I try not to be obvious, but when his friends come over,
> I look them over stealthily and most of them are cutting,"
> said Andy's mother. "You can see the scars in the summer
> when they wear shorts or short sleeves."

Most kids outgrow this behavior, but don't ignore it or dismiss it as a phase. Without overreacting, ask your child the reasons for the behavior, and don't fall into the trap of invalidating them ("It could be worse—you could be a Syrian refugee!") which could make your child feel even worse. Intervene if the behavior continues. If your child doesn't yet have a therapist, now is the time to get one. You can also help by working together on a plan for what to do instead of self-harm, when emotions feel intolerable. Talk about the ways you've learned to deal with your own stress.

Handling Violence at Home

As we've noted, sometimes depression can make adolescents, particularly boys, irritable and aggressive. Sometimes this leads to violence.

A child with uncontrollable anger is crying out for limits, and for you to show you can keep everyone safe. Establish rules when things are calm. Make it clear that if anyone becomes physically violent, you will leave the house and call the police, and then stick to that rule the first time it happens: no freebies. It's also a good idea to prepare a list of emergency phone numbers and post it in a prominent place, reinforcing the fact that you mean business.

If you get any inkling that your child's illness could lead to violence, research the options in your community. You may be surprised by how much help is available. Some cities have crisis services that offer temporary, 24-hour care, short of hospitalization. But this may not be an option if your child is seriously aggressive.

One of the most important things you'll need to do if there's a threat of violence is to manage your own reactions. Revealing your fear, anger, or anxiety can fan the flames of your child's emotions, setting the two of you up for a dangerous feedback loop. A rule for doctors in Samuel Shem's book *House of God* is: "At a cardiac arrest, the first procedure is to take your own pulse." Check in with yourself and keep calm so that you can assess the situation, think clearly, and resist the impulse to yell or hit, which could frighten your child and escalate the danger. Recall the stress-management tips and do's and don'ts of dealing with conflicts we provided in Chapter 5, and practice telling yourself: *I am the adult here.* In the thick of things, you want to be able to scan the environment to make sure there aren't any dangerous items the child could grab and harm anyone. If you do see something, try to calmly remove it while keeping an eye on the child.

"We have a mantra at home, which a wise friend once taught me," says Beth. "It's 'Don't let your lizard brain take over your wizard brain.'"

Beth makes a key point. If your adolescent flies into a rage, he or she is reacting with the most primitive part of the brain, the one involved in life-or-death struggles. The prefrontal cortex, involved in reasoning and good judgment, is the newest to evolve, and the one that separates us from most animals. It's still under construction in your child until about age 25. Sometimes you'll need to use your evolutionary advantage.

This may be a major test of your empathy. If things have reached this point, your child is telling you that he or she is out of control and needs you to keep things safe. You might say something like: "I see how upset you are and want to help. I'm going to stay with you and make sure you stay safe. When you're ready, I want to know what is bothering you. Can you try to take some deep breaths and tell me what's wrong?"

If you can't get the behavior under control in a reasonable amount of time, don't hesitate to call for help. Sometimes your spouse or another adult close to the child may be better able to defuse the situation. If need be, however, call your child's doctor, a therapist, Child Protective Services, or a community mental health agency. Or if there's no other option, call 911, with the guidance we offer below.

Flights From Reason

A very small percentage of children with depression—less than five in every hundred—at some point will see or hear things that aren't real. This is known as psychosis and may be a sign that the illness is worsening. Hallucinations and delusions might include hearing voices, most commonly—particularly negative, critical comments—to seeing monsters or a scary character from a movie. These could be triggered by stress, a new medication, recreational drugs, seizures, migraines, infections, bipolar mania, or schizophrenia. Your child will likely be frightened and may be reluctant to tell you about these experiences. But if you see signs of this occurring, call your clinician right away.

You may suspect your child has taken a hallucinogen, such as LSD or mushrooms. No matter how you feel about these drugs, it's important not to behave aggressively. If the problem is not due to drugs, your child's doctor may want to prescribe a medication to treat the psychosis.

Call the Cops?

If all else fails, you may need to call 911. In many parts of the country, local governments don't have adequate funds for mental health response teams, meaning police are your only alternative for a response in a crisis.

Sometimes all it takes to change a child's out-of-control behavior is for a uniformed cop to arrive and ask some pointed questions. Police can also transport a person who needs to go to the hospital, even if they are opposed.

On the other hand, depending on where you live, you may want to think twice before enlisting local police in a mental health emergency. Sometimes officers can skillfully handle such crises. In others, however, they can make a volatile situation worse—even deadly. In fact, about half of the people who are killed by police have some sort of disability, according to a Ruderman Family Foundation report analyzing incidents from 2013 to 2015. One of the cases investigated involved Kristiana Coignard, 17, who walked into the lobby of an East Texas police station asking for help. Coignard, who reportedly struggled with depression, had a knife in her waistband and "I have a gun" written on her hand. A scuffle with officers ended in her death.

If you have a child at risk of serious violence at home, we recommend that you waste no time in introducing yourself to local police in advance of a possible crisis and assessing whether you can depend on their help. If you can't, make sure you have another, better emergency plan.

If You Do Call 911 . . .

- Relay the information as calmly as you can.
- Use the phrase "mental health crisis" and explain the diagnosis.
- Ask if a crisis intervention team (CIT) is available. These are officers who have been specially trained to deal with this kind of emergency.
- When the officer arrives, repeat that you've called about a mental health crisis.
- Don't panic if you see your child escorted out in hand-cuffs. But make sure to get the name of the officer and, if possible, follow the car.

The 988 Alternative

Remember this number. It's designed to be easy to do so.

In July 2020, the Federal Communications Commission (FCC) designated 988 to replace the old 10-digit number for the National Suicide Prevention Lifeline. The service's new name is "988 Suicide & Crisis Lifeline," and calls are answered by staff trained in suicide counseling and other mental health and substance-use-related emergencies. 988 services are also available by SMS (just by texting, you guessed it, 988).

The switch was inspired by both the recent rise in suicide attempts and several incidents in which police were not prepared to respond. If you call or text 988, you may still be routed to the police, but in most cases it won't be necessary. A survey of Lifeline centers found police weren't required in about 98% of the calls, while in the remaining 2%, the caller was able to collaborate with Lifeline services to coordinate the response.

At this writing, it's too early to tell how this new program may work. Another alternative for advice by phone is Parents Anonymous's national helpline, at 1-855-4APARENT (1-855-427-2736), with counselors available from 10 a.m. to 7 p.m. PST. Many states have other helplines.

Crises at School

One of the most upsetting news stories in recent years concerned 15-year-old Ethan Crumbley, arrested in 2021 for shooting four people at a high school in Rochester Hills, Michigan. Teachers had previously caught the boy looking for ammunition online and drawing scenes of violence with the words "help me." In a highly unusual move by law enforcement, Crumbley's parents were also arrested and charged in the crime, for giving their son a gun and ignoring signs of his mental distress.

School shootings are rare, and Ethan's parents were clearly outliers, as subsequent reporting established. They not only ignored signs of their child's mental illness and refused the school's request to take him home, but fled from police after being charged. So what lessons can more reasonable adults draw from the case?

Perhaps most importantly, understand that you can't count on every school to do the right thing when your child or someone else's child is in a crisis. There was a lot of debate after the Crumbley killings as to whether school officials should have acted more decisively. (When they couldn't get the parents' cooperation, they returned the boy to his class.) You should expect that if a student is clearly losing control that he or she will be removed from class, at least temporarily. If you get this kind of call from school, you should be ready to respond quickly, and take your child to see a clinician ASAP. If not, you may risk having the school send your child to the hospital in a police car, an obviously traumatic experience.

> "I got a call from my daughter's school in October, telling me she was planning to harm herself and that I was immediately required to remove her from school," says Janet. "From that moment on, she was with another adult, a teacher or the school psychologist, at all times. But before I could get there, the school resource officer had stepped in and decided the right course of action was for her to go to a mental health facility. Had I not agreed, they would have transported her without my consent."

Trouble With the Law

It's—alas—not entirely unlikely that at some point you're going to be dealing with police. Your child may even end up incarcerated. Estimates vary widely, but one study suggested that up to 7 out of 10 youth in juvenile hall have some sort of diagnosable mental health problem.

There are some obvious reasons for this. Especially in boys, depression can often lead to aggressiveness and even conduct disorder, while the hopelessness accompanying depression can diminish care about the consequences of antisocial behavior.

Juvenile justice in some ways is like the adult system, with parallel rules for arrests, hearings, and probation. But theoretically, at least, it operates on the premise that youth are less responsible for their actions and more responsive to rehabilitation than adults. We say "theoretically" because attitudes vary from place to place and even from person to person. No matter how ill your child may be, you can't count on universal understanding and tolerance.

If your child has been causing nonstop conflict at home, it may be tempting not to fight against detention for the sake of some relief. It's also true that some kids from chaotic home environments might benefit from the extra structure, rules, consequences, and regular meals. But for most adolescents with mental illnesses, you'll want to avoid or limit the time in detention as much as you can. Juvenile hall is no place for someone coping with depression, as just one statistic makes clear: Incarcerated youth die by suicide two to three times more often than those in the general population.

Juvenile hall "counselors," who also serve as guards, are normally not well-trained to deal with mental illness, despite how common it is in that environment. They will often mistake mood disorder symptoms as defiance and punish it accordingly. Solitary confinement isn't uncommon, even as many states are challenging it, and no matter how traumatizing it can be to someone struggling with mental illness. There's also a risk that your child will receive psychotropic drugs that you or their doctor wouldn't want them to take. Finally, being around law-breaking and sometimes violent kids not only physically endangers your kid but makes it more likely he or she will be influenced to continue antisocial behavior.

"About half of our juvenile hall is a mental health facility. And we don't have adequate services to keep up with that," Arthur L. Bowie, supervising assistant public defender of Sacramento County's juvenile division, told a reporter in 2014. "We're making criminals out of them."

Police have a lot of discretion if they arrest your child. Sometimes if you appear at the station as an obviously concerned and responsible parent, you can talk them out of a formal arrest. This unfortunately is one way the justice system penalizes the poor: Kids whose parents can't get time off their jobs to attend to them or find a good lawyer will likely face harsher treatment.

Know Your Rights

The juvenile justice system is large, complex, and constantly changing. We have room for just a few of the basics in this book. By now, however, we hope you've gotten good at googling. Many local communities and states have nonprofit organizations that will help you advocate for your child. The relevant words and phrases to find them are "juvenile justice," "advocacy," "mental illness," and the name of your state. We also list some online resources for you at the end of this book.

You should know that police must notify you if and where they are detaining your son or daughter. They may decide to send your child home with you but with a notice to later appear at the station or in court. If your child is sent to juvenile hall, he or she has the right to make at least two phone calls, one of which must be to a lawyer.

Sometimes the stay will be brief, the charges minor, and for juveniles you can expect that the arrest record will later be sealed and expunged. But for anything more serious, you'll want to find an attorney, either for pay or pro bono—or you may be assigned one from the public defender's office. Make sure to notify your child's doctor ASAP and request that he or she attest to your child's mental health issues and alternatives to detention.

As soon as you can, find a contact person at the hall and make that person aware of your child's mental health challenges. Advise them if your child is taking medication and get that medication to the hall without delay. You may find yourself needing to educate your child's lawyer, if there is one, about depression/bipolar disorder. It's also a good idea to provide psychiatric and educational evaluations to court personnel and your attorney. If your son or daughter has an individualized education program (IEP) or 504 plan, provide that to your contact at the hall and inform your child's attorney. Any existing accommodations should apply to any educational services provided in detention.

For serious charges, a juvenile court judge may decide on one of several possible outcomes:

- Your child may be sent back to live with you under court supervision.
- Your child may be sent to live in a group home, institution, or foster home.
- Your child may be put on probation and sent to a program, which may be out of state.
- Your child may be sent to a juvenile correctional facility.

- In the most serious cases, such as homicide, rape, and crimes with guns, and if your child is older than 14, he or she may be tried as an adult and sent to prison. In that case, he or she will stay at a juvenile justice facility until at least age 18.

As the parent or guardian of your child, you may be financially responsible for any damages caused, including court-ordered payments to any victims.

Desperate Means

Now we come to that hardest of topics, the scariest for any parent to consider, but one you must face and prepare for if your child is seriously depressed. Whether or not your child has made a suicide attempt in the past or has talked about doing so, this is a danger you can't afford to ignore.

> "We understood it was serious after she confided to the school psychologist that she had five or six ways she was thinking about to kill herself," says Janet. "She had some super-detailed thoughts that showed she'd done some research . . . Later I found it was written all over her planners, and on her laptop. I had no idea until I searched her room."

Many depression-related suicides occur during the first few episodes of illness, before a person has learned that the hopeless feelings and suicidal thoughts will eventually pass. This is one reason why adolescents, who don't yet have much life experience dealing with their symptoms, are at greater risk of acting on their suicidal impulses. Most suicidal adolescents desperately want to live but can't see another way out of their intolerable distress. Treatment can provide them with a life-affirming means of working toward getting well.

Risk Factors

A child is considerably more likely to attempt suicide if:

- There's a family history of such behavior
- There are guns in the house
- The child is LGBTQ+ and has gotten negative feedback about "coming out"
- The child has an eating disorder or is abusing drugs
- A girl has been a victim of sexual abuse

Among older teenagers, girls are twice as likely as others to make a suicide attempt, but boys are four times more likely to die by suicide. Up to half of those who ultimately die by suicide have made previous attempts. In fact, most deaths from suicide are preceded by warning signs that survivors may recognize only after the fact. (See the list below for some clues.)

Red Flags

Here are some warning signs that your child may be at risk of suicide:

- Withdrawal from friends, family, and activities
- Violently rebellious behavior, or running away
- An increase in risk-taking behavior
- Drug or alcohol use
- Unusual neglect of his or her appearance
- Describing himself or herself as a bad person

- Saying things like "Nothing matters anymore," or "I won't be a problem much longer"
- Giving away prized possessions, throwing out important belongings, or otherwise putting his or her affairs in order
- Becoming cheerful overnight after a period of depression
- Having hallucinations or bizarre thoughts

Discouraging Suicidal Behavior

As we've noted throughout this book, it's crucial to have regular talks with your child and be aware of what's going on in his or her life. Without overdoing it, don't be afraid to address your worries. You might say something like, "I can tell you've been under some stress lately" and ask if there's any way to help. You might also say "I worry because I love you" and ask if things ever get so hard that your child has thought about suicide. If your child is not already in treatment, this may be the time to start. If your child insists that he or she is fine, gently leave the door open to talk again about this in the future. Yet this is one of those occasions when you really don't want to be too subtle.

> "Words gain strange and mystical powers when they are not spoken at times when they should be spoken," writes Rep. Raskin. "Not talking about suicide to a depressed person is like not talking about sex and birth control to a teenager. Verbal taboos create mystery, and people gravitate toward mystery . . . as uncomfortable and intrusive as it may seem, it is essential to use the word *suicide* itself in order to demystify and deflate it, to strip it of its phony pretense to omnipotence and supernatural force."

Don't be afraid to say that scary word, especially if your child knows someone who has died by suicide or has seen recent media coverage of it. Young people are vulnerable to "suicide contagion"—an increase in suicidal thoughts and behavior triggered by news, gossip, and idealization of a person who has just died by suicide. That's why Netflix changed the controversial suicide scene in the TV series *13 Reasons Why* two years after the show's 2017 premiere. Experts warned that the depiction of the lead actress cutting her wrist with a razor blade may have encouraged copycats.

You can't control everything your child watches or hears. But you can keep your ears open and use these occasions to have a frank conversation. You might ask what other action the friend or fictional character might have taken in response to adversity.

You've probably heard that saying about suicide being a permanent solution to a temporary problem. Many young people die by suicide impulsively after a stressful event such as losing a pet or being humiliated in some way, such as being ostracized at school, getting in trouble with the law, or breaking up with a girlfriend or boyfriend. If your child is open to talking about suicidal thoughts, suggest that you can collaborate to prevent it. Some parents and children have worked together to produce a safety plan that stipulates warning signs, coping strategies, and resources—including other adults your child can call. What activities always make your child feel better? Does he or she know you can be called at work or anywhere else?

If your child is seriously depressed, don't delay doing the safety sweep we described in Chapter 5. It's essential and worth repeating that you should get rid of or lock up any guns and knives and prescription medications.

Hospitalization

Kids with severe depression will sometimes need to be hospitalized, especially if they have attempted suicide or are threatening to do so.

Your child may be sent to a hospital after a crisis at school or a brush with police, or after a clinician recommends it. You should also consider requesting hospitalization if your child can no longer function at school or in public. A significant upside is that you can count on your child being physically safe for as long as it lasts. Moreover, on discharge, the staff should present you with a plan for continued outpatient care. Sometimes they will recommend community resources you didn't know existed.

> "The only bright light in Lisa's hospitalization was the social worker who hooked us up with a very good halfway house, where Lisa gradually improved enough after a few months to come home," says Lisa's mother, Sheila.

Prepare a contingency plan for hospitalization as soon as you know your child has a serious mood disorder. Find the best available facility, based on what you can learn about its quality of care and whether it's in-network under your insurance plan. If possible, look for a teaching hospital, where you can count on an experienced psychiatrist overseeing the residents and other staff treating your child. Check whether the hospital is accredited by the Joint Commission on Accreditation of Healthcare Organizations (JCAHO).

If your child needs a hospital stay, starting it sooner rather than later may expedite treatment. Be sure to introduce yourself to not only the team that will be treating your child during the day but also to the evening staff. You should visit your child in the hospital during different times of the day so that as many of the staff as possible knows who you are and that they should call you with any problems.

Having your child be hospitalized can be frightening, especially if it's the first time and you have no idea what to expect. There's nothing like inpatient care, moreover, to press home the reality of your child's illness.

Don't hesitate to press doctors to keep you informed. You have a right to information about the treatment being given to your child. Be clear with the hospital treatment team that you expect them to get your consent to any medication decision— even in the middle of the night.

If you're calling to check in on your child and can't get through, keep calling until you do, even if you must explain your problem to the first operator you talk to and ask for help in escalating your request. One option is to talk to the patient relations department, which every hospital should have.

If a time comes when you believe your child is stable and don't agree with continued hospitalization, and if your child agrees, you can ask to have your child released. But if the medical team disagrees with this, a court hearing may be necessary.

Do your best to connect the inpatient team caring for your child with the outpatient team that will take up the work when your child is released.

It's a good idea to ask that the two teams have a conference call, with you included, to discuss next steps.

Affording the Hospital Stay

Once again ideally, you should understand your insurance plan benefits *before* your child needs serious care. Call the number on your insurance card and get an explanation. Make sure to ask about what happens if your child needs repeated hospital stays. If the answer isn't satisfactory, look into other plans.

If your child has already been hospitalized, notify your plan right away and inquire about the cost. If the hospital is not in your plan's network, alert them that you want them to negotiate a rate with your insurance company. If you don't have adequate insurance coverage at the time your child is hospitalized, consider applying for Medicaid.

The average length of a psychiatric hospitalization is between 7 and 13 days, and can sometimes be longer, but in recent years it's becoming ever-shorter. Your insurance company will likely push for the briefest possible stay, while the hospital staff may push back, if needed. Still, understand that the hospital's goal will be to stabilize the patient, solving the acute crisis. Don't expect intensive psychotherapy. Medication, group therapy, and family crisis intervention will be the main tactics. Visits with the psychiatrist may last less than half an hour per day, if that.

What If Your Child Doesn't Consent to Hospitalization?

Many parents are surprised to learn that their child under age 18 has the right to refuse treatment, including hospitalization. The nature of the rights and the age at which they begin vary from state to state. But it's good to be aware that you may find yourself in a situation where your child's psychiatrist recommends hospitalization, and you agree, but your child doesn't consent.

In such cases, most states allow a physician to prescribe involuntary hospitalization for a short evaluation period, usually three days. After that time, if the evaluation team believes that a longer hospitalization is needed, a court hearing is required to determine whether the child can be forced to stay in the hospital. If the team recommends involuntary admission, the court can issue an order for a specific period.

The Lure of the "Troubled Teen" Industry

"Ellen left for a treatment program one month after her suicide attempt," says Charlene. "Faced with her depression, intrusive thoughts and constant suicidal ideations, and close to zero help from our health plan, I just couldn't do it at home anymore."

Imagine your child is out of control: breaking rules, staying out all night, and maybe even violent. You fear that he or she is taking dangerous drugs and hanging out with dangerous people. Like Charlene, you may also feel the medical system has let you down.

You're at your wits' end. You're in trouble at work for all the time you've had to take off to care for your kid. Your other children may also be starting to act out. You're arguing with your partner. And then someone tells you that you can send your rebellious adolescent away somewhere—by force, if need be—for a few months for intensive treatment, discipline, and care. It may cost a fortune and insurance may not pay a dime, but you'll get a reprieve and your child may get life-changing therapy. Who wouldn't be tempted?

A growing and lucrative "troubled teen" industry, focused on problems including addiction, has emerged to respond to this yearning. More than 5,000 adolescents a year end up in "wilderness therapy" camps like the one Ellen attended, according to a 2020 investigative report on the industry in *Undark.*

In most cases, a child will move on from three months or more in a wilderness camp to a longer period in a residential treatment center (RTC) or boarding school that is often run by the same company. At last count there were more than 170 "therapeutic boarding schools," and many hundreds of "residential treatment centers" and private and government-run camps including the one Ellen attended. (Precise numbers aren't available, since not all facilities are licensed.) There's also a parallel transport business, sometimes staffed by buff military veterans, to escort resistant patients to their new quarters.

The camps, many located in Utah and other western states, draw inspiration from the Outward Bound youth adventure program founded in Wales in 1941. But unlike Outward Bound, they combine psychotherapy and boot-camp-style discipline to address serious adolescent behavorial problems. Ellen had to learn to sew her own backpack and carve her own spoon before she could eat. The *Undark* report quoted other kids who had to remove their shoes and shout their names while using the toilet, to prevent them from running away.

Some families say they feel lucky to have found well-run wilderness-and-residential programs to fill a desperate need.

> "I watched several students turn their lives around," says the journalist David Marcus, who spent 18 months observing a group of adolescents attending a wilderness camp and boarding school for his book, *What It Takes to Pull Me Through: Why Teenagers Get in Trouble—and How Four of Them Got Out.* "These programs don't work miracles, but some kids just need a chance to reflect, to

confront themselves and their demons, while their parents do the same," Marcus says.

At the same time, however, Marcus and other observers worry about the overall industry tendency to regard teens as a revenue stream. What's more, staff turnover, uneven curriculums, and patchy state standards have led to programs of vastly varying quality. The staff issues, aggravated by pandemic labor turmoil, could undermine children's safety.

Most of the programs are also extremely expensive. Wilderness camps can cost more than $500 a day for several weeks on top of several thousand dollars more for admission fees, plus at least a couple thousand dollars more for an "escort." RTCs and therapeutic boarding schools may cost as much as $10,000 a month. Educational counselors who direct parents to programs tack on another couple of thousand.

Insurance coverage is iffy at best, although you'll most likely be reimbursed if you choose a more conventional RTC, offering short-term (six months or less) intensive therapy in a locked facility. For boarding schools, insurance plans may cover only the hours spent in therapy. For wilderness camps, plans rarely if ever reimburse, and sometimes specifically exclude them. That's largely due to the lack of strong scientific evidence that they make a difference. At this writing, wilderness therapy had yet to be subjected to a randomized controlled trial, with replicable results.

"It's hard to make a case for spending a lot of money on a program for which there is no strong evidence," John Weisz, a professor of psychology at Harvard University who specializes in mental health interventions for children and adolescents, told *Undark*, adding, "From the state of the evidence that I've seen, we really don't know whether wilderness therapy has beneficial effects or not."

Wilderness programs in particular have a dark recent history. In 2007, a General Accounting Office report investigated thousands of allegations of abuse, including some fatalities, at programs throughout the country. These included the deaths of a 16-year-old girl who fell while rock climbing and a 14-year-old boy who died from dehydration.

Again, we do understand the fear and sense of urgency that would push a parent to opt for these programs. But at this writing, we're concerned about both the risks and expense. Added to everything else, you should consider the risk that your child may never forgive you.

> After Ellen returned from her four-month wilderness experience, her mother said: "Combined with the medication, the program helped, overall, but we got a different kid back. It was as if she no longer quite trusted us."

Maybe you're in the kind of crisis where you feel there's no alternative, and maybe—we hope—you've found a reputable program. Still, consider these suggestions:

- *Don't cut off communication with your child.* The best programs include parent participation. Choose one that allows you to visit at will and which guarantees regular updates on your child.
- *Make sure the program is licensed by the state in which it's based.* Then ask to see that license or contact the licensing agency. You can also check with the Better Business Bureau.
- *Do even more due diligence.* Ask your child's doctor about the program and request references from successful graduates.

- *Vet the staff.* The clinical director should have stellar credentials and experience treating depression, and the program should have qualified and licensed therapists on board. Don't sign up with any facility that won't provide information on background checks of staff.
- *Investigate the academic curriculum if you're looking at more than three months.* Avoid having your child fall behind in school if possible.
- *Visit the site.* And ask for a tour. Ensure that the facility is safe—with adequate security—and sanitary; if possible, observe staff interactions with the kids.

We can probably assume most readers of this book haven't reached this point of urgency, and we hope none of you do. But however desperate you may feel at this moment, keep in mind that it will pass. If you stick to evidence-based treatment while providing loving support at home, the odds are good that your child will emerge from this phase intact—and quite possibly much better.

Conclusion

Hope on the Horizon

We've spent much of this book preparing you for some of the worst things that can happen if your son or daughter is moderately to seriously depressed. Yet we hope what you'll keep foremost in mind are the very good chances that your child will do just fine. Depression is a manageable illness. Millions of adults who've been diagnosed with it are leading lives with the same chance of happiness and fulfillment as anyone else. David Sheff writes, "We increase our pain because we compare our insides with other people's outsides. It looks as if everyone else is doing great, that their kids are sailing through—but no one is sailing through. When we choose not to hide our struggles, there is tremendous relief. We can be supported. We can get help. We learn that we aren't alone. And we aren't. We are in this together."

In the time we've spent working on this book, we've heard of many lives that have changed for the better.

When we last checked in on Ruby Walker, the 15-year-old who dropped out of school due to depression and wrote a book about it, she was 20 years old, living with her mom, stepdad, and brother, and studying art and creative writing at Trinity University in San Antonio, Texas. She had also dyed her hair pink. "The sad shit's over," she declared on her website.

Chamique Holdsclaw, the professional basketball star who struggled with depression at age 11, was diagnosed with bipolar disorder in 2011, and inducted into the Women's Basketball Hall of Fame seven years later. At this writing, she is devoting her time to mothering her two young children and speaking about mental health in schools and other venues. Part of her mission is to counter the resistance she still sees in Black and Brown communities to get help. "I say, listen, there's no need to walk around in pain; there are resources and organizations to help you. Let's do some digging. You can move through this." Public speaking isn't easy for her, she says, "but I'm passionate about this. If I can help give kids a foothold, I'm all for it."

After several years of crises, including being hospitalized while in college, Lisa Himmel, now in her mid-30s, lives on her own, works for a medical services company, and feels more in control of her moods and her eating disorder. "Treatment and recovery has not been smooth or linear," she wrote us. "It's been a journey and if I were to put a number on it, this was a 17-year battle. Now, I feel more balanced . . . I love fitness and that has been a blessing, especially over Covid. I also love walking and running and one of my daily joys is taking my sweet dog, Leon, for walks and runs. I feel as if the past two years have given me a chance to really get to know myself and what I like, don't like, what qualities had been buried from the disorder. . . . I'm happy for the most part. I have an amazing family and gratitude."

Matt was in his mid-20s, with a girlfriend he loves, an interesting job, and a close relationship with his mother, Beth, who had once called the police to take him to school. When Beth recently asked him how he felt about that morning, she was happily surprised by his answer. "You overreacted," he said. "But at least you were paying attention."

Maria, who at 15 was cutting herself and talking about suicide, had learned skills to manage her anxiety and depression and was "getting stronger every day," said her mother, Lourdes. "Early intervention with highly qualified doctors got us to this point," Lourdes added. "Ever since she got treated, when we ask how she is feeling, she is emotionally equipped to provide feedback and say 'I am ok,' or 'feeling sad,' which she was not able to do before treatment. She will tell us if she feels the need for additional help."

In some cases, parents remained wary. "We have rebuilt as much as we can so far and she hasn't self-harmed in nine months," reported Charlene, whose daughter Ellen was hospitalized after a suicide attempt. "Currently, she's at a good and stable point. It feels nice to just ride along smoothly for a moment. But I'm still afraid anytime we approach a bump in the road."

For Charlene and many other parents, we see abundant reason to have faith that your child will get through this and get better. The pandemic has done unquestionable damage to many US children's mental health, disrupting routines, increasing social isolation, and for some, even costing them their parents and other elders. Yet by worsening a crisis already underway, this catastrophe may have caused a tipping point in which society finally rises to this challenge.

Progress on Policies

Already today, kids with all kinds of mental illness are on average being identified and treated earlier than ever, potentially meaning that they can be helped before their brains get into harmful ruts. Urged on by advocates, legislators have been seeking ways to better regulate social media firms purveying emotionally harmful content. And new initiatives are starting to address the nationwide shortage of psychotherapists, including school psychologists.

In December 2021, the US Surgeon General, Vivek Murthy, issued a rare public advisory, calling on parents, researchers, social media executives, philanthropists, employers, and journalists to combat what he called a devastating epidemic.

"We cannot overlook the escalating mental health crisis facing our patients," American Academy of Pediatrics President Lee Savio Beers said earlier that year. "We must treat this mental health crisis like the emergency it is."

At this writing, the US Congress was considering major bills to boost funding for children's mental health services. Some state governments have also joined the fight. Several have been seeking ways to improve access to mental health care, while California's governor recently signed a law requiring health insurers to provide services within 10 business days.

Some states are also trying at last to help kids get more sleep. In 2022, California became the first state to mandate that high schools start no earlier than 8:30 a.m. and middle schools no earlier than 8 a.m.

To address the shortage of child psychiatrists, four US medical centers recently unveiled a new program allowing pediatricians to become board-certified adult and child psychiatrists in just three years instead of the usual five.

Insurance companies, while still not abiding by the spirit of mental health parity, have been expanding access to mental health care in at least some ways, such as by approving reimbursements for phone and computer-based therapeutic sessions.

News From the Labs

Scientists are working on several promising fronts. In 2015, US researchers launched the ABCD Study, the nation's largest-ever long-term inquiry into children's brain development and health. The federally funded project enrolled nearly 12,000 students of diverse races, ethnicities, and education and income levels. Research tools will include brain scans and extensive, repeated interviews to try to understand the relationship between factors such as sleep, substance use, and physical activities with mental health. By observing brain development through adolescence and beyond, the study may identify contributors to mood disorders and lead to improved diagnosis and treatment.

Other scientists are seeking new treatments for depression. Psychedelic substances such as psilocybin and LSD have shown initial promise in adults, while ketamine has been effective in at least one small study of adolescents. Scientists are also excited by new clues about the role of the immune system and systemic inflammation as the origin of many psychiatric disorders.

Building on the promise of transcranial magnetic stimulation (TMS), described in Chapter 3, researchers are also seeking to develop more sophisticated ways of stimulating brain regions to ease depression. In October 2021, the *American Journal of Psychiatry* published results of a small study in which 80% of participants had their depression go into remission after treatment with SAINT, for Stanford Accelerated Intelligent Neuromodulation Therapy. The treatment is a type of TMS that uses "theta burst stimulations," a process that typically lasts a total of only three to four minutes. In the 2021 study, participants had 10 sessions a day every day for five days.

Scientists are tracking down genes that increase the risk of depression, with the hope that one day, genetic tests and maybe also brain scans may help diagnose mental illness and pinpoint the right treatment for each individual.

The Slow Revolution in Our Schools

It can be hard to recognize historic transformation when you're living through it, but these past several years have brought steady change in the field of education. Much of this progress could make life much easier for kids with mental challenges—and in fact, for all kids and their families.

We've told you about the federal laws that provide accommodations for students who need them. There are also important societal changes underway, including an increasing questioning of the value of higher education. The pandemic poured fuel on this attitude adjustment when most colleges turned to remote learning. But the questioning has been going on for many years.

One signpost of the change was the 2006 bestseller *The Price of Privilege*, in which psychologist Madeline Levine investigated what she characterized as an epidemic of emotional problems, including skyrocketing rates of depression, substance use, and anxiety disorders, sabotaging America's most privileged young people. Levine contended that upper-middle-class materialism, intrusive parenting, and pressure to achieve had created a toxic brew resulting in the highest rates of adolescent mood disorders in any socioeconomic sector.

Four years later came the breakout popular success of *Race to Nowhere*, a documentary that touched on the same themes. Tens of thousands of Americans throughout the country crowded into school auditoriums to hear its messages, hanging around afterward for public discussions of the damage done by pressuring kids into unrestrained résumé-building. First-time filmmaker Vicki Abeles said she resolved to investigate the problem after a doctor told her that her 12-year-old daughter was having stress-induced stomachaches. She interviewed students who told her about their insomnia, anxiety, and prevalent cheating. The film's basic message is that kids' mental health suffers when success is defined by high grades and test scores.

The nonprofit Challenge Success, which we mentioned in Chapter 7, arose in the wake of the reaction to Levine's book and Abeles's movie. It has since worked with hundreds of schools and families, championing reforms such as:

- *New attention to students' schedules*, including later start days, limits on homework, and moving finals to before winter break
- *Modified grading systems*, such as using narrative assessments and eliminating student rankings, while implementing stronger policies against cheating
- *Adult education*, including "dialogue nights" in which students share concerns with parents and faculty, and efforts to "de-bunk the myth that there is only one path to success"

All over the United States, individual schools and school districts have been paying more attention to students' emotional well-being. One small example is the new Wellness Center at

Archie Williams High School in San Anselmo, California: a cozy room with sofas, tea, fidgets, and two welcoming full-time staff. The center provides temporary respite for kids who are feeling overwhelmed, while attempting to reduce the rising rates of "school refusal." "There was some pushback when the idea for this came up six years ago, as we were in the midst of budget cuts," says assistant principal Chad Stuart. "But it has been a terrific investment and now other schools in the county are looking into doing this as well."

Still Needed: More Focus on the Really Big Picture

Even with all the new progress in labs, schools, and even legislatures, we all need to think harder about broader, structural issues that have huge and inequitable impacts on mental health. Better health insurance won't be much use to a parent who can't get time off from a job to drive a child to therapy. Improved telehealth won't help a family that can't afford WiFi. A new "wellness" center is of limited support for a child who can't sleep in a crowded, noisy apartment. These are just some of the long-festering problems that will take enormous political will to improve, yet which would surely deliver huge benefits for everyone's mental health.

How to Hang in There

You may be using every bit of energy you have right now to help your child manage this illness. Yet you may want to consider, now or later, extending your efforts to support some of the progress being made in mental health. Maybe you'll create a small parents' support group at your school. Maybe you'll send money to an advocacy group you admire. Maybe you'll write your congressional representative to champion a mental health bill. Maybe you'll run for office yourself—there are so many problems that need solving. You've learned so much about this illness, and humans in general, by caring for your child. At some point you may want to capitalize on your experience to help support others.

If you're still in the thick of it, however, remember that you're not alone, and that there are many resources out there to support you and your family. We offer lists of books and websites at the end of this book, and we encourage you to be relentless in taking advantage of them.

Remember, too, that your child is so much more than any issues he or she may have. One of the best things you can do as a parent will be to see and reflect back that bigger picture, highlighting all the gifts your unique child brings to the world.

Appendix

Antidepressant Medications for Adolescents

Primary and Secondary Line of Treatments	
Selective Serotonin Reuptake Inhibitors	
FDA Approved	**Dose Range/Day**
Fluoxetine (Prozac)*	20 to 60 mg
Escitalopram (Lexapro)	10 to 20 mg
Off-Label Use	
Citalopram (Celexa)	20 to 40 mg
Fluvoxamine (Luvox)*	50 to 200 mg
Paroxetine (Paxil)	10 to 50 mg
Sertraline (Zoloft)*	50 to 200 mg
Also FDA approved for obsessive-compulsive disorder in children and adolescents.	
Tertiary Line of Treatments	
Serotonin Norepinephrine Reuptake Inhibitors	
Off-Label Use	**Dose Range/Day**
Duloxetine (Cymbalta)*	30 to 120 mg
Desvenlafaxine (Pristiq)	50 to 100 mg
Levomilnacipran (Fetzima)	40 to 120 mg
Venlafaxine XR (Effexor)	150 to 225 mg
Also FDA approved for generalized anxiety disorders in children and adolescents.	

227

Other Antidepressants Used Off-Label	
Off-Label Use	**Dose Range/Day**
Bupropion (Wellbutrin)	100 to 300 mg
Trazodone (Desyrel)	100 to 150 mg
Vortioxetine (Trintellix)	10 to 20 mg
Vilazodone (Vibryd)	10 to 40 mg
Mirtazapine (Remeron)	15 to 45 mg

Adapted from *Depression: Parents' medication guide—AACAP*. (n.d.). Retrieved August 31, 2022, from https://www.aacap.org/App_Themes/AACAP/docs/resource_centers/resources/med_guides/DepressionGuide-web.pdf

Education

504 or IDEA: What's the Difference?

Who's Covered?

IDEA

- All school-aged children meeting criteria for one or more of 14 conditions, including "emotional disturbance" and depression
- Children whose disabilities adversely affect educational performance

SECTION 504

- Students meeting the definition of physically or mentally "handicapped" in ways that "substantially limit" a life activity, such as walking, seeing, hearing, speaking, and learning

How Are Students Evaluated?

IDEA

- Requires that the child be fully and comprehensively evaluated by a multidisciplinary team
- Requires informed and written parental consent
- Requires a re-evaluation of the child at least once every three years, or if conditions warrant or if the child's parent or teacher requests it

SECTION 504

- Requires a variety of documented sources
- Parents need to be notified but written consent isn't required.
- Requires "periodic" re-evaluation
- No provisions made for independent evaluation at school's expense
- Requires re-evaluation before a significant change in placement

What Services Are Guaranteed?

IDEA

- Requires an individualized education program (IEP)
- Provides any combination of special education and general education classrooms
- Provides related services, if required, which might include speech and language therapy, occupational therapy, physical therapy, counseling services, psychological services, social services, and transportation

SECTION 504

- Does not require an IEP, but does require a plan
- Provides an education comparable to that provided to those students who are not disabled
- Placement is usually in a general education classroom. Children can receive specialized instruction, related services, or accommodations within the general education classroom.
- Provides related services, if needed

What If Parents and Schools Disagree?

IDEA

- Must provide impartial hearings for parents who disagree with the identification, evaluation, or placement of the student
- An impartial appointee selects a hearing officer.
- The student's current IEP and placement continues to be implemented until all proceedings are resolved.
- Parents must receive 10 days' notice prior to any change in placement.
- Enforced by US Department of Education, Office of Special Education

Section 504

- Must provide impartial hearings for parents who disagree with the identification, evaluation, or placement of the student
- Requires that parents have an opportunity to participate and be represented by legal counsel
- A hearing officer is usually appointed by the school.
- Enforced by US Department of Education, Office of Civil Rights

Source: deBettencourt, L. U. (2002). Understanding the differences between IDEA and Section 504. *TEACHING Exceptional Children*, *34*(3), 16-23. https://doi.org/10.1177/004005990203400302. Reproduced with permission.

Sample Gebser Letter

Send individual letters to both the school principal and superintendent.

Your name

Date

Dear (name of school principal and school district superintendent):

I am writing you on behalf of my child, (name and birthdate), who is a student attending (name of high school) in the (name of school district).

My son/daughter, who has been diagnosed with (insert name of the disability), is being repeatedly discriminated against (or bullied), prohibiting him/her from being able to access his/her education. (Detail how the student is not able to access education—school refusal, unable to ride the bus, etc.) We have already alerted the following school personnel to the issue: (list of names). But it has not been addressed.

The (name of school district) receives federal funds in return for which it contracts to not discriminate. It is your legal requirement to investigate and correct this discrimination. School administrators have control over the site and personnel involved. If you do not investigate and correct the problem, you and the district are acting in a way that implies you are deliberately indifferent to the discrimination. You and the school district may be liable personally and officially for damages.

I request that you (insert what you think will solve the problem for your child).

Optional bullying language:

The (name of school district) has an anti-bullying policy that states: (insert specifics that have been violated).

As you can see from the examples I have given you, this anti-bullying policy is not being upheld.

I would appreciate your written notification, of when I can expect the investigation to be complete and what steps you will be taking, within 10 days. Please put a copy of this letter in my child's cumulative file.

Sincerely,

(Your name)

Note: Thanks to Catherine Michael of the CMK Law Firm in Carmel, Indiana, for this wording.

Glossary

504 plan A set of classroom accommodations to support students who need help short of special education.

adrenal glands Glands located just above the kidneys. Their hormones help regulate many physiological functions, including the body's stress response.

adrenocorticotropic hormone (ACTH) A hormone released by the pituitary gland.

anticipation A genetic pattern in which there is a tendency for individuals in successive generations to develop hereditary disorders at earlier ages and with more severe symptoms.

antidepressant A medication used to prevent or relieve depression.

antipsychotic A medication used to prevent or relieve psychotic symptoms. Some newer antipsychotics have mood-stabilizing effects as well.

anxiety disorder Several mental health disorders in the category of anxiety that are characterized by significant or maladaptive feelings of tension, fear, or worry.

attention-deficit/hyperactivity disorder (ADHD) A disorder characterized by a short attention span, excessive activity, or impulsive behavior. The symptoms of the disorder begin early in life.

atypical depression A form of major depression or dysthymia in which the person is able to cheer up when something good happens, but then sinks back into depression once the positive event has passed.

bipolar disorder A mood disorder characterized by an overly high mood, called mania, which alternates with depression.

catatonia A state of severely disordered activity characterized by physical immobility, purposeless overactivity, extreme negativism, refusal to speak, parrot-like echoing of someone else's words, or mimicking of another's movements.

Children's Health Insurance Program (CHIP)   A partnership between the federal and state governments that provides reduced-cost health coverage to children in families earning too much money to qualify for Medicaid.

chronic depression   A form of major depression in which symptoms are present continuously for at least two years.

clinical psychologist   A mental health professional who provides assessment and therapy for mental health and emotional disorders.

cognitive-behavioral therapy (CBT)   A form of psychotherapy that aims to correct ingrained patterns of thinking and behavior that may be contributing to a person's mental health, emotional, or behavioral symptoms.

comorbidity   The simultaneous presence of two or more disorders.

conduct disorder   A disorder characterized by a repetitive or persistent pattern of having extreme difficulty following rules or conforming to social norms.

corticotropin-releasing hormone   A substance released by the hypothalamus.

cortisol   A hormone released by the adrenal glands that is responsible for many of the physiological effects of stress.

crisis residential treatment services   Temporary, 24-hour care in a nonhospital setting during a crisis.

delusion   A belief that is seriously out of touch with reality.

depression   A feeling of being sad, hopeless, or apathetic that lasts for at least a couple of weeks. *See* major depression.

***Diagnostic and Statistical Manual of Mental Disorders*, 5th ed. (*DSM-5*)**   The manual that mental health professionals use for diagnosing all kinds of mental illnesses.

dopamine   A neurotransmitter that is essential for movement and also influences motivation and perception of reality.

dysthymia   A mood disorder that involves being either mildly depressed or irritable most of the day. These feelings occur more days than not for 12 months or longer and are associated with other symptoms.

eating disorder   A disorder characterized by serious disturbances in eating behavior. People may severely restrict what they eat or binge-eat and then attempt to compensate by such means as self-induced vomiting or misuse of laxatives.

electroconvulsive therapy (ECT)   A rarely used treatment that involves delivering a carefully controlled electrical current to the brain, producing a brief seizure.

family therapy   Psychotherapy that brings together members of a family for therapy sessions.

frontal lobes   Part of the brain involved in planning, reasoning, controlling voluntary movement, and turning thoughts into words.

gamma-aminobutyric acid (GABA)   A neurotransmitter that inhibits the flow of nerve signals in neurons by blocking the release of other neurotransmitters.

group therapy   Psychotherapy that brings together several patients with similar diagnoses or issues.

hallucination   The sensory perception of something that isn't really there.

health maintenance organization (HMO)   A type of managed care plan in which members must use health care providers who work for the HMO.

hippocampus   Part of the brain that plays a role in learning, memory, and emotion.

home-based services   Assistance provided in a patient's home to improve family coping skills and avert the need for more intensive services.

hospitalization   Inpatient treatment in a facility that provides intensive, specialized care and close, round-the-clock monitoring.

hypothalamic-pituitary-adrenal (HPA) axis   A body system comprising the hypothalamus, pituitary gland, and adrenal glands along with the substances these structures secrete.

hypothalamus   Part of the brain that serves as the command center for the nervous and hormonal systems.

individual therapy   Psychotherapy in which a patient meets one on one with a therapist.

individualized education program (IEP)   A written educational plan for a student qualifying for major support under IDEA.

Individuals with Disabilities Education Act (IDEA)   A federal law that applies to students who have a disability affecting their ability to benefit from general educational services.

interpersonal therapy (IPT)   A form of psychotherapy that aims to address the interpersonal triggers for emotional or behavioral symptoms.

Katie Beckett option   *See* TEFRA option.

kindling hypothesis   A theory stating that repeated episodes of mania or depression may spark long-lasting changes in the brain, making it more sensitive to future stress.

learning disorder   A disorder that adversely affects a person's performance in school or ability to function in everyday situations that require reading, writing, or math skills.

light therapy   A therapeutic regimen of daily exposure to bright light from an artificial source.

major depression   A mood disorder that involves either being depressed or irritable nearly all the time or losing interest or enjoyment in almost everything. These feelings last for at least two weeks, are associated with several other symptoms, and cause significant distress or impaired functioning.

managed care   A system for controlling health care costs.

mania   An overly high or irritable mood that lasts for at least a week or leads to unusual and potentially dangerous behavior. Symptoms include grandiose ideas, decreased need for sleep, racing thoughts, risk-taking, and increased talking or activity. These symptoms cause marked impairment in functioning or relationships.

manic depression   *See* bipolar disorder.

Medicaid   A government program, paid for by a combination of federal and state funds, that provides health and mental health care to low-income individuals who meet eligibility criteria.

melancholia   A severe form of major depression in which there is a near-complete absence of interest or pleasure in anything.

melatonin   A hormone that regulates the body's internal clock, controlling rhythms of sleep, body temperature, and hormone secretion.

mental health parity   A policy that attempts to equalize the way that mental and physical illnesses are covered by health plans.

mental illness   A mental disorder characterized by abnormalities in mood, emotion, thought, or higher-order behaviors, such as social interaction or the planning of future activities.

mood   A pervasive emotion that colors a person's worldview.

mood disorder   A mental health disorder in which a disturbance in mood is the chief feature.

neuron   A cell in the brain or another part of the nervous system that is specialized to send, receive, and process information.

neurotransmitter   A chemical that acts as a messenger within the brain.

norepinephrine   A neurotransmitter that plays a role in the body's response to stress and helps regulate arousal, sleep, and blood pressure.

omega-3 polyunsaturated fatty acids   A substance found in foods, including cold-water fish, such as salmon and tuna, flaxseed, walnuts, and pecans. Omega-3s have anti-inflammatory properties, which may help with symptoms of depression.

oppositional defiant disorder   A disorder characterized by a persistent pattern of unusually frequent defiance, hostility, or lack of cooperation.

partial hospitalization   Services such as individual and group therapy, special education, vocational training, parent counseling, and therapeutic recreational activities that are provided for at least four hours per day.

point of service (POS) plan   A type of managed care plan that is similar to a traditional HMO or PPO, except that its members can also use providers outside the HMO organization or PPO network in exchange for a higher co-payment or deductible.

preferred provider organization (PPO)   A type of managed care plan in which members may choose from a network of providers who have contracts with the PPO.

prefrontal cortex   Part of the brain involved in complex thought, problem-solving, and emotion.

protective factor   A characteristic that decreases a person's likelihood of developing an illness.

psychiatrist   A medical doctor who specializes in the diagnosis and treatment of mental illnesses and emotional problems.

psychosis   A state of severely disordered thinking characterized by delusions or hallucinations.

psychotherapy   The treatment of a mental, emotional, or behavioral disorder through "talk therapy" and other psychological techniques.

randomized controlled trial   A study in which participants are randomly assigned to a treatment group or a control group. The control group receives either a placebo or standard care. This study design allows researchers to determine which changes in the treatment group over time are due to the treatment itself.

recurrence   A repeat episode of an illness.

relapse   The re-emergence of symptoms after a period of remission.

remission   A return to the level of functioning that existed before an illness.

residential treatment center   A facility that provides round-the-clock supervision and care in a dorm-like group setting. The treatment is less specialized and intensive than in a hospital, but the length of stay is often considerably longer.

resilience   The ability to adapt well to stressful life events and bounce back from adversity, trauma, or tragedy.

respite care   Child care provided by trained parents or mental health aides to give the usual caregivers a short break.

reuptake   The process by which a neurotransmitter is absorbed back into the sending branch of the nerve cell that originally released it.

risk factor   A characteristic that increases a person's likelihood of developing an illness.

S-adenosyl-L-methionine (SAMe)   A natural compound that is sold as a dietary supplement.

schizoaffective disorder   A severe form of mental illness in which an episode of either depression or mania occurs at the same time as symptoms of schizophrenia.

schizophrenia   A severe form of mental illness characterized by delusions, hallucinations, or serious disturbances in speech, behavior, or emotion.

seasonal affective disorder (SAD)   A form of major depression in which the symptoms start and stop around the same time each year. Typically, they begin in the fall or winter and subside in the spring.

selective serotonin reuptake inhibitor (SSRI)   A widely prescribed class of antidepressants.

self-efficacy   The belief in one's own ability to perform effectively in a particular situation.

serotonin   A neurotransmitter that plays a role in mood and helps regulate sleep, appetite, and sexual drive.

side-effect   An unintended effect of a drug.

social rhythm therapy   A therapeutic technique that focuses on helping people regularize their sleep and daily routines.

St. John's wort (*Hypericum perforatum*) An herb sold as a dietary supplement, with purported benefits for depression.

stress   The physiological response to any perceived threat—real or imagined, physical or psychological.

substance use disorder   The continued use of alcohol or other drugs despite negative consequences, such as dangerous behavior while under the influence or substance-related personal, social, or legal problems.

suicidality   Suicidal thinking or behavior.

switching   The rapid transition from depression to hypomania or mania.

synapse   The gap that separates nerve cells.

system of care   A network of mental health and social services that are organized to work together to provide care for a particular patient and his or her family.

TEFRA option   A funding option, authorized by the Tax Equity and Financial Responsibility Act of 1982, that allows states to provide community- and home-based services for children with disabilities who are living at home and need extensive care.

temperament   A person's inborn tendency to react to events in a particular way.

transcranial magnetic stimulation (TMS)   An experimental treatment in which a special electromagnet is placed near the scalp, where it delivers short bursts of energy to stimulate the nerve cells in a specific part of the brain.

utilization review   A formal review of health care services by a managed care plan to determine whether payment for them should be authorized or denied.

Resources

Books

General Information for Parents

Treating and Preventing Adolescent Mental Health Disorders: What We Know and What We Don't Know
Editors: Dwight L. Evans, Edna B. Foa, Raquel E. Gur, Herbert Hendin, Charles P. O'Brien, Daniel Romer, Martin E. P. Seligman, and B. Timothy Walsh
Publisher: Oxford University Press; 2nd edition, 2017

Straight Talk About Your Child's Mental Health: What To Do When Something Seems Wrong
Author: Stephen V. Faraone
Publisher: The Guilford Press, 2003

The Explosive Child: A New Approach for Understanding and Parenting Easily Frustrated, Chronically Inflexible Children
Author: Ross W. Greene, PhD
Publisher: Quill, 2001

The Stressed Years of Their Lives: Helping Your Kid Survive and Thrive During Their College Years
Authors: B. Janet Hibbs, PhD, MFT, and Anthony Rostain, MD, MA
Publisher: First St. Martin's Griffin edition, 2020

Mood Prep 101: A Parent's Guide to Preventing Depression and Anxiety in College-Bound Teens
Author: Carol Landau
Publisher: Oxford University Press, 2020

Depression for Dummies
Authors: Laura L. Smith and Charles H. Elliott
Publisher: For Dummies; 2nd edition, 2021

The Brain
Neuroscience for Dummies
Author: Frank Amthor
Publisher: For Dummies; 2nd edition, 2016

The Teenage Brain: A Neuroscientist's Survival Guide to Raising Adolescents and Young Adults
Authors: Frances E. Jensen with Amy Ellis Nutt
Publisher: Harper Paperbacks; Reprint edition, 2016

The Three-Pound Enigma: The Human Brain and the Quest to Unlock Its Mysteries
Author: Shannon Moffett
Publisher: Algonquin Books, 2006

Personal Accounts of Depression
Reasons to Stay Alive
Author: Matt Haig
Publisher: Penguin Life, 2016

Monochrome Days: A First-Hand Account of One Teenager's Experience With Depression
Authors: Cait Irwin, Dwight L. Evans, MD, and Linda Wasmer Andrews
Publisher: Oxford University Press, 2007

Acquainted With the Night: A Parent's Quest to Understand Depression and Bipolar Disorder in His Children
Author: Paul Raeburn
Publisher: Broadway Books, 2004

Unthinkable: Trauma, Truth, and the Trials of American Democracy
Author: Jamie Raskin
Publisher: Harper, 2022

Lincoln's Melancholy: How Depression Challenged a President and Fueled His Greatness
Author: Joshua Wolf Shenk
Publisher: Mariner Books, 2006

The Golden Ticket: A Life in College Admissions
Author: Irena Smith
Publisher: SheBooks, 2023

His Bright Light: The Story of Nick Traina
Author: Danielle Steel
Publisher: Delacorte Press, 1998

Darkness Visible: A Memoir of Madness
Author: William Styron
Publisher: Random House, 1990

The Noonday Demon: An Atlas of Depression
Author: Andrew Sullivan
Publisher: Scribner, 2002

Just Like Someone Without Mental Illness Only More So: A Memoir
Author: Mark Vonnegut
Publisher: Bantam, 2011

Especially for Adolescents
When Nothing Matters Anymore: A Survival Guide for Depressed Teens
Author: Bev Cobain
Publisher: Free Spirit Publishing; Revised and updated edition, 2007

Depression Is the Pits, But I'm Getting Better: A Guide for Adolescents
Author: E. Jane Garland
Publisher: Magination Press; 1st edition, 2010

Conquering the Beast Within: How I Fought Depression and Won . . . and How You Can, Too
Author: Cait Irwin
Publisher: Three Rivers Press, 1999

The Thought That Counts: A Firsthand Account of One Teenager's Experience With Obsessive-Compulsive Disorder
Authors: Jared Kant, Martin Franklin, PhD, and Linda Wasmer Andrews
Publisher: Oxford University Press, 2008

Ups and Downs: How to Beat the Blues and Teen Depression
Authors: Susan Klebanoff, PhD, and Ellen Luborsky, PhD
Publisher: Price Stern Sloan, 1999

Wide Awake: A Buddhist Guide for Teens
Author: Diana Winston
Publisher: TarcherPerigee, 2003

Bipolar Disorder
If Your Adolescent Has Bipolar Disorder: An Essential Resource for Parents
Authors: Dwight L. Evans, MD, Tami D. Benton, MD, and Katherine Ellison
Publisher: Oxford University Press, 2023

Bipolar Disorder for Dummies
Author: Candida Fink and Joe Kraynak
Publisher: For Dummies; 3rd edition, 2015

Mind Race: A Firsthand Account of One Teenager's Experience With Bipolar Disorder
Authors: Patrick E. Jamieson, PhD, with Moira A. Rynn, MD
Publisher: Oxford University Press, 2006

The Bipolar Teen: What You Can Do to Help Your Child and Your Family
Authors: David J. Miklowitz and Elizabeth L. George
Publisher: The Guilford Press, 2007

ADHD
Buzz: A Year of Paying Attention
Author: Katherine Ellison
Publisher: Hachette Books, 2010

Driven to Distraction
Authors: Edward M. Hallowell and John J. Ratey
Publisher: Anchor, 2011

ADHD: What Everyone Needs to Know
Authors: Stephen Hinshaw and Katherine Ellison
Publisher: Oxford University Press, 2015

If Your Adolescent Has ADHD
Authors: Thomas J. Power, PhD, and Linda Wasmer Andrews
Publisher: Oxford University Press, 2018

*What Your ADHD Child Wishes You Knew: Working Together to Empower Kids for
    Success in School and Life*
Author: Sharon Saline, MD
Publisher: TarcherPerigee, 2018

The Essential Guide to Raising Complex Kids With ADHD, Anxiety, and More
Author: Elaine Taylor-Klaus
Publisher: Fair Winds Press, 2020

Anxiety
*You and Your Anxious Child: Free Your Child From Fears and Worries and Create a
    Joyful Family Life*
Authors: Anne Marie Albano and Leslie Pepper
Publisher: Avery, 2013

If Your Adolescent Has an Anxiety Disorder: An Essential Resource for Parents
Authors: Edna B. Foa, PhD, and Linda Wasmer Andrews
Publisher: Oxford University Press, 2006

What You Must Think of Me: A Firsthand Account of One Teenager's Experience With Social Anxiety Disorder
Authors: Emily Ford, Michael Liebowitz, and Linda Wasmer Andrews
Publisher: Oxford University Press, 2007

Eating Disorders

Next to Nothing: A Firsthand Account of One Teenager's Experience With an Eating Disorder
Authors: Carol Arnold with B. Timothy Walsh, MD
Publisher: Oxford University Press, 2007

Hungry: A Mother and Daughter Fight Anorexia
Authors: Sheila Himmel and Lisa Himmel
Publisher: Berkley; Original edition, 2009

Eating Disorders: What Everyone Needs to Know
Authors: B. Timothy Walsh, Evelyn Attia, and Deborah R. Glasofer
Publisher: Oxford University Press, 2020

If Your Adolescent Has an Eating Disorder: An Essential Resource for Parents
Authors: B. Timothy Walsh, MD, and Deborah R. Glasofer
Publisher: Oxford University Press; 2nd edition, 2020

Schizophrenia

If Your Adolescent Has Schizophrenia: An Essential Resource for Parents
Authors: Raquel E. Gur, MD, PhD, and Ann Braden Johnson, PhD
Publisher: Oxford University Press, 2006

Me, Myself, and Them: A Firsthand Account of One Young Person's Experience With Schizophrenia
Authors: Kurt Snyder, Raquel E. Gur, MD, PhD, and Linda Wasmer Andrews
Publisher: Oxford University Press, 2007

Self-Harm

Night Falls Fast: Understanding Suicide
Author: Kay Redfield Jamison
Publisher: Knopf, 1999

Cutting: Understanding and Overcoming Self-Mutilation
Author: Steven Levenkron
Publisher: W. W. Norton & Company; Revised edition, 1999

Eight Stories Up: An Adolescent Chooses Hope Over Suicide
Authors: DeQunicy Lezine and David Brent
Publisher: Oxford University Press, 2008

Substance Use Disorders

Chasing the High: A Firsthand Account of One Young Person's Experience With Substance Abuse
Authors: Kyle Keegan and Howard Moss
Publisher: Oxford University Press, 2008

Clean: Overcoming Addiction and Ending America's Greatest Tragedy
Author: David Sheff
Publisher: HarperCollins, 2013

Beautiful Boy: A Father's Journey Through His Son's Addiction
Author: David Sheff
Publisher: Mariner Books, 2018

High: Everything You Want to Know About Drugs, Alcohol, and Addiction
Authors: David Sheff and Nic Sheff
Publisher: HarperCollins, 2019

Tweak: Growing Up on Methamphetamines
Author: Nic Sheff
Publisher: Atheneum Books for Young Readers, 2009

School

Special Education—Plain and Simple: A Quick Guide for Parents, Teachers, Advocates, Attorneys, and Others
Author: Patricia L. Johnson Howey
Publisher: Beyond the Sunset Publisher; 2nd edition, 2021

Wrightslaw: From Emotions to Advocacy: The Special Education Survival Guide
Authors: Pamela Wright and Peter Wright
Publisher: Harbor House Law Press; 2nd edition, 2006

Wilderness Camps, Residential Treatment, and Boarding Schools

What It Takes to Pull Me Through: Why Teenagers Get in Trouble—and How Four of Them Got Out
Author: David L. Marcus
Publisher: Harper Paperbacks; Reprint edition, 2006

Help at Any Cost: How the Troubled-Teen Industry Cons Parents and Hurts Kids
Author: Maia Szalavitz
Publisher: Riverhead Books, 2006

Additional Resources

Parenting Helplines
National: https://www.nationalparenthelpline.org/
State Lists: https://www.nationalparenthelpline.org/find-support/state-resources
Parents Anonymous national helpline: 1-855-4A PARENT/(1-855-427-2736)

Foundations
National and International Professional, Advocacy, and Research Groups
American Academy of Child and Adolescent Psychiatry
3615 Wisconsin Avenue, N.W.
Washington, DC 20016-3007
202-966-7300
http://www.aacap.org

American Foundation for Suicide Prevention
AFSP National Office
199 Water Street
11th Floor
New York, NY 10038
(888) 333-AFSP (2377)
https://afsp.org/

American Psychiatric Association
800 Maine Avenue, SW, Suite 900
Washington, DC 20024
(202) 559-3900
https://www.psychiatry.org/

American Psychological Association
750 First Street NE
Washington, DC 20002-4242
(800) 374-2721
https://www.apa.org/

Depression and Bipolar Support Alliance
55 E Jackson Blvd, Suite 490
Chicago, IL 60604
(800) 826-3632
https://www.dbsalliance.org/

Activist Groups
Bring Change to Mind
https://bringchange2mind.org/

Families for Depression Awareness
https://www.familyaware.org/

Make It OK
https://makeitok.org/

One Mind
https://onemind.org/

National Alliance on Mental Illness
4301 Wilson Blvd., Suite 300
Arlington, VA 22203
1-800-950-6264
http://www.nami.org

Mental Health America – Depression
https://www.mhanational.org/conditions/depression

JED Foundation
530 7th Avenue, Suite 801
New York, NY 10018
(212) 647-7544
https://jedfoundation.org/

LGBTQ+
The Trevor Project
Call 1-866-488-7386 toll-free

***Helping Families Support Their Lesbian, Gay, Bisexual, and Transgender
    (LGBT) Children***
Author: Caitlin Ryan, PhD, ACSW
https://nccc.georgetown.edu/documents/LGBT_Brief.pdf

People of Color
The Steve Fund
P.O. Box 9070
Providence, RI 02940
info@stevefund.org
(401) 249-0044
https://www.stevefund.org/

Online Information for Parents
AACAP Facts for Families
https://www.aacap.org/AACAP/Families_and_Youth/Facts_for_Families/Layout/
    FFF_Guide-01.aspx

Adolescent Brain Cognitive Development
https://abcdstudy.org/

Beyond Differences
https://www.beyonddifferences.org/

Centers for Disease Control and Prevention
The CDC offers a broad array of health information, including a page about Positive
Parenting Practices: www.cdc.gov/healthyyouth/protective/positiveparenting/
index.htm

Columbia University Clinic for Anxiety and Related Disorders
https://www.anxietytreatmentnyc.org/specialized-programs.cfm

Coping Cat Parents
An online resource center for parents that provides high-quality, evidence-based
information on anxiety and its treatment
https://www.copingcatparents.com/Helping_Kids

Depression: True Stories
A video series that includes an interview with Chamique Holdsclaw, featured in
the book.
https://vimeo.com/ondemand/depressiontruestories

Effective Child Therapy: Evidence-based mental health treatment for children and
adolescents
https://effectivechildtherapy.org/

Employee Assistance Programs
https://www.workplacementalhealth.org/mental-health-topics/employee-assista
nce-programs

Food and Drug Administration: The site includes material on vaping, smoking,
cannabis, CBD, COVID, and dietary supplements.
www.fda.gov

International Society of Interpersonal Psychotherapy – ISIPT
https://interpersonalpsychotherapy.org/

MedlinePlus: Teen Depression
https://medlineplus.gov/teendepression.html

National Institute of Mental Health
https://www.nimh.nih.gov/

**Parents' Medication Guides (American Academy of Child and Adolescent
Psychiatry)**
https://www.aacap.org/AACAP/Families_and_Youth/Family_Resources/Parents_
Medication_Guides.aspx?hkey=c5ad9d72-b5db-4994-b3ab-96fe5350439a

Protecting Youth Mental Health
The US Surgeon General's Report, 2021
https://www.hhs.gov/sites/default/files/surgeon-general-youth-mental-health-
advisory.pdf

Society for Adolescent Mental Health and Medicine
https://www.adolescenthealth.org/Resources/Clinical-Care-Resources/Mental-Health/Mental-Health-Resources-For-Parents-of-Adolescents.aspx

Find a Provider

The National Alliance on Mental Illness (NAMI) has a helpline for free assistance Monday through Friday, 10 a.m. to 10 p.m. EST. You can reach the helpline at 1-800-950-6264. NAMI also offers a free, 24/7 crisis text: just text 988.

The Substance Abuse and Mental Health Services Administration (SAMHSA), a government agency, provides a treatment locator for low-cost facilities.
https://findtreatment.gov/

The National Association of Free & Charitable Clinics, Mental Health America, and the Open Path Psychotherapy Collective also provide online tools to find affordable mental health services.
https://nafcclinics.org/
https://mhanational.org/finding-help
https://openpathcollective.org/find-a-clinician/

Psychology Today—probably hands-down the easiest way to locate a therapist or psychiatrist, you can search by insurance, location, etc.
https://www.psychologytoday.com/us

Find a CBT Therapist (Association for Behavioral and Cognitive Therapies)
https://services.abct.org/i4a/memberDirectoryus/index.cfm?directory_id= 3&pageID= 3282

Child and Adolescent Psychiatrist Finder (American Academy of Child and Adolescent Psychiatry)
https://www.aacap.org/AACAP/Families_and_Youth/Resources/CAP_Finder.aspx

Talkspace
https://www.talkspace.com/

BetterHelp
https://www.betterhelp.com/

NATSAP—The National Association of Therapeutic Schools and Programs provides information on licensed facilities.
https://natsap.org/

Health Insurance

The Children's Health Insurance Program (CHIP)
https://www.healthcare.gov/medicaid-chip/childrens-health-insurance-program/

Employee Benefits Security Administration: Ask EBSA
https://www.dol.gov/agencies/ebsa/about-ebsa/ask-a-question/ask-ebsa

HealthCare.gov
https://www.healthcare.gov/

HealthSherpa
https://www.healthsherpa.com/

Medicaid: Managed Care
https://www.medicaid.gov/medicaid/managed-care/index.html

Reimbursify
https://reimbursify.com/

Internet Management
Children's Online Privacy Protection Rule ("COPPA")
https://www.ftc.gov/legal-library/browse/rules/childrens-online-privacy-protection-rule-coppa

ConnectSafely—extremely useful and up-to-date information for parents on the latest online platforms kids are using.
https://www.connectsafely.org/parentguides

Parenting, Media, and Everything in Between (Common Sense Media)
https://www.commonsensemedia.org/articles

A Parent Guide to Teens, Technology, & Social Media
Author: Karen Hamilton, LMFT, CATC
A useful guide for parents regarding teens, tech, and social media:
https://karenhamiltontherapy.com/wp-content/uploads/2018/09/A-Parent-Guide-to-Teens-Technology-Social-Media-2018-new.pdf

Cyberbullying Research Center
https://cyberbullying.org/
They have handouts with tips for parents and teens, and a resource section that also includes advice for parents about sexting.

Wait Until 8th
https://www.waituntil8th.org/

Suicide Prevention
988 Suicide & Crisis Lifeline
Offers free and confidential emotional support in crisis. National network local crisis centers answer calls 24-7.
https://988lifeline.org/
988

American Foundation for Suicide Prevention
AFSP National Office

199 Water Street
11th Floor
New York, NY 10038
(888) 333-AFSP (2377)
https://afsp.org/

JED Foundation
530 7th Avenue, Suite 801
New York, NY 10018
(212) 647-7544
https://jedfoundation.org/

The Steve Fund
P.O. Box 9070
Providence, RI 02940
info@stevefund.org
(401) 249-0044
https://www.stevefund.org/

Substance Use Disorders

Alcoholics Anonymous
(212) 870-3400 (check your phone book for a local number), www.aa.org

American Council for Drug Education
www.acde.org

Beautiful Boy Fund
https://www.beautifulboyfund.org/

Leadership to Keep Children Alcohol Free
(937) 848-2993 www.alcoholfreechildren.org

Narcotics Anonymous
(818) 773-9999, www.na.org

National Council on Alcoholism and Drug Dependence
www.ncadd.us

National Institute on Alcohol Abuse and Alcoholism
(301) 443–3860, www.niaaa.nih.gov

National Institute on Drug Abuse
(301) 443-6441, https://nida.nih.gov/

Partnership to End Addiction
(212) 841-5200, https://drugfree.org/

Substance Abuse and Mental Health Services Administration
(800) 662-4357, www.samhsa.gov

Education
Wrightslaw
https://www.wrightslaw.com/
You can also contact a Parent Training and Information Center in your state, which offers free information on special-needs education.

Matrix Parent Network and Resource Center for families of children with special needs
https://www.matrixparents.org/

Academic Accommodations for Students With Psychiatric Disabilities
https://www.washington.edu/doit/academic-accommodations-students-psychiatric-disabilities

Boston University's NITEO Program
https://cpr.bu.edu/wellness-and-recovery-services/niteo/

Challenge Success
https://challengesuccess.org/

Fountain House College Re-Entry
https://collegereentry.org/

Road2College: Colleg Co-Op Programs: What You Need to Know
https://www.road2college.com/colleges-with-coop-programs/

Scholarships.com: Clinically Depressed Scholarships
https://www.scholarships.com/financial-aid/college-scholarships/scholarship-directory/physical-disabilities/clinically-depressed

Homeschooling
https://www.highschoolofamerica.com/
Learn more about homeschooling and how your child can earn a recognized diploma from High School of America today.

Job Corps
https://www.jobcorps.gov/parents

Gap year programs
https://www.gapyearassociation.org/
The Gap Year Association

Bullying
StopBullying.gov
https://www.stopbullying.gov/

Beyond Differences
https://www.beyonddifferences.org/

Juvenile Justice
Youth.gov
https://youth.gov/youth-topics/juvenile-justice

Navigating the Juvenile Justice System in New Jersey: A Family Guide
https://www.njjn.org/uploads/digital-library/NJ-Parents-Caucus_Navigating-JJ-
System-Family-Guide_2014.pdf

ADHD
Children and Adults with Attention-Deficit/Hyperactivity Disorder (CHADD)
4221 Forbes Blvd, Suite 270
Lanham, MD 20706
(301) 306-7070, http://www.chadd.org

Learning Disorders and Disabilities
International Dyslexia Association
(410) 296-0232, www.interdys.org

LD OnLine
www.ldonline.org

Learning Disabilities Association of America
(412) 341-1515, www.ldaamerica.org

National Center for Learning Disabilities
(301) 966-2234, www.ncld.org

YAI—Seeing Beyond Disability
https://www.yai.org/
This organization along with affiliate agencies offer support and services for children and adults with intellectual and developmental disabilities.

US Department of Justice ADA Information Line
For information on government support, call 800-514-0301 or go to www.ada.gov

Eating Disorders
National Association of Anorexia Nervosa and Associated Disorders
(888) 375-7767, www.anad.org

National Eating Disorders Association
1-800-931-2237, www.nationaleatingdisorders.org

Free Apps to Chart Moods
Note: Before using any app:
1. Check for price changes; these are all free, but there are "premium" paid options.

2. Make note of the free trial period's duration, if applicable.
- T2 Mood Tracker
  Monitors moods for: anxiety, stress, depression, brain injury, posttraumatic stress, and general well-being.
- eMoods
  eMoods can help identify triggers for a relapse of depression.
- Moodpath
  After an initial screening, this app provides a "scientifically validated" assessment every two weeks.

Mental Health Law
Americans With Disabilities Act
https://www.ada.gov/

Colorado General Assembly: Children and Youth Mental Health Treatment Act
https://leg.colorado.gov/bills/hb18-1094

Council of Parent Attorneys and Advocates
https://www.copaa.org/

US Equal Employment Opportunity Commission: Questions and Answers on the Final Rule Implementing the ADA Amendments Act of 2008
https://www.eeoc.gov/laws/guidance/questions-and-answers-final-rule-implementing-ada-amendments-act-2008

US Department of Labor: Family and Medical Leave Act
https://www.dol.gov/agencies/whd/fmla

Parity

The Mental Health Parity and Addiction Equity Act (MHPAEA)
https://www.cms.gov/CCIIO/Programs-and-Initiatives/Other-Insurance-Protections/mhpaea_factsheet
To check your health plan's compliance with parity, call or go to the following:

US Department of Labor Employee Benefits Security Administration (EBSA)
https://www.dol.gov/agencies/ebsa—check page on consumer information on health plans or contact EBSA toll-free at 1-866-444-3272

US Department of Health and Human Services: 1-877-267-2323 ext. 61565

National Association of Insurance Commissioners
https://content.naic.org/
Contains your state's department of insurance website and contact information.

To learn more about benefits and the appeals process, go to:

The National Conference of State Legislatures: Mental Health Benefits: State Laws Mandating or Regulating https://www.ncsl.org/research/health/mental-health-benefits-state-mandates.aspx

The HealthCare.gov page on health insurance rights and protections.

The US Department of Labor maintains a parity resource webpage with links to the federal parity regulations, "Frequently Asked Questions" and other agency guidance, educational fact sheets, videos, reports, and links to other websites and organizations with helpful parity information. https://www.dol.gov/agencies/ebsa/laws-and-regulations/laws/mental-health-and-substance-use-disorder-parity

Community Catalyst and Health Law Advocates posts a wide range of health care resources, including resources for substance use disorders advocates and resources for healthcare consumers. www.communitycatalyst.org, www.healthlawadvocates.org

Helpful handout on parity: https://www.communitycatalyst.org/resources/publications/document/parity-issue-brief-FINAL-12-9-14.pdf?1418154547

Bibliography

Abeles, V., & Congdon, J. (Directors). (2010). *Race to nowhere* [Film]. Reel Link Films.

Adolescent Brain Cognitive Development. (n.d.). *About the study.* https://abcdst udy.org/about/

American Academy of Child and Adolescent Psychiatry. (2019, October). *Marijuana and teens.* https://www.aacap.org/AACAP/Families_and_Youth/Fac ts_for_Families/FFF-Guide/Marijuana-and-Teens-106.aspx

American Academy of Child and Adolescent Psychiatry. (n.d.). *Post pediatric portal programs.* https://www.aacap.org/AACAP/Medical_Students_and_Residents/ Triple_Board_Residency_Training/Post_Pediatric_Portal_Programs.aspx

American Academy of Pediatrics. (2014). School start times for adolescents. *Pediatrics, 134*(3), 642–649. https://doi.org/10.1542/peds.2014-1697

American Academy of Pediatrics, the American Academy of Child Adolescent Psychiatry, & the Children's Hospital Association. (2021, October 19). *Pediatricians, child and adolescent psychiatrists and children's hospitals declare national emergency in children's mental health.* https://www.aap.org/en/news-room/news-releases/aap/2021/pediatricians-child-and-adolescent-psychiatri sts-and-childrens-hospitals-declare-national-emergency-for-childrens-mental-health/

American Foundation for Suicide Prevention. (n.d.). *An introduction to firearms and suicide prevention.* https://afsp.org/an-introduction-to-firearms-and-suicide-prevention

American Psychiatric Association. (2018). *Position statement on the risks of adolescents' online activity.* https://www.psychiatry.org/getattachment/fb0fcd5b-45d5-4177-9756-47a35f389048/Position-2018-Risk-of-Adolescents-Online-Activ ity.pdf

American Psychiatric Association. (2022). *Diagnostic and statistical manual of mental disorders* (5th ed., text revision).

American Psychological Association. (2017). *Parenting styles.* https://www.apa.org/act/resources/fact-sheets/parenting-styles

Axelson, D. (2019). Meeting the demand for pediatric mental health care. *Pediatrics, 144*(6), Article e20192646. https://doi.org/10.1542/peds.2019-2646

Bailey, R. K., Mokonogho, J., & Kumar, A. (2019). Racial and ethnic differences in depression: Current perspectives. *Neuropsychiatric Disease and Treatment, 15,* 603–609. https://doi.org/10.2147/NDT.S128584

Baltz, J. W., & Le, L. T. (2020). Serotonin syndrome versus cannabis toxicity in the emergency department. *Clinical Practice and Cases in Emergency Medicine, 4*(2), 171–173. https://doi.org/10.5811/cpcem.2020.1.45410

Barr, L. (2020, January 10). Five minutes with Ruby Walker, formerly depressed teen. *Texas Lifestyle Magazine.* https://texaslifestylemag.com/lifestyle/five-minutes-with-ruby-walker-formerly-depressed-teen/

Berge, J. M. (2009). A review of familial correlates of child and adolescent obesity: What has the 21st century taught us so far? *International Journal of Adolescent Medicine and Health, 21*(4), 457–483. https://doi.org/10.1515/ijamh.2009.21.4.457

Bogost, I. (2018, October 29). The fetishization of Mr. Rogers's "look for the helpers." *The Atlantic.* https://www.theatlantic.com/technology/archive/2018/10/look-for-the-helpers-mr-rogers-is-bad-for-adults/574210/

Boston Children's Health Physicians. (2019, August 12). *Growing trend of school refusal.* https://www.childrenshospital.org/bchp/news/growing-trend-school-refusal

Brody, D. J., & Gu, Q. (2020, September). Antidepressant use among adults: United States, 2015–2018. *NCHS Data Brief, 377.* https://www.cdc.gov/nchs/products/databriefs/db377.htm

Brown, B. (2019, August 7). *What Toni Morrison taught me about parenting.* https://brenebrown.com/articles/2019/08/07/what-toni-morrison-taught-me-about-parenting/

Bulik, B. S. (2017, March 20). *Doctors in New Zealand—The only non-U.S. country that allows DTC advertising—Call for bans.* Fierce Pharma. https://www.fiercepharma.com/marketing/doctors-new-zealand-only-other-country-allows-dtc-advertising-hate-it-too

Campbell, D. (2018, December 11). Study finds high levels of depression among LGB teenagers. *The Guardian.* https://www.theguardian.com/world/2018/dec/12/study-finds-high-levels-of-depression-among-lgbt-teenagers

Caron, C. (2021, September 21). Worried about your teen on social media? Here's how to help. *The New York Times.* https://www.nytimes.com/2021/09/21/well/family/teens-social-media-help.html

CBS News. (2021, November 7). *SAINT: Hope for new treatment of depression.* https://www.cbsnews.com/news/saint-treatment-for-depression/

Centers for Disease Control and Prevention. (n.d.). *CDC healthy schools: Obesity.* https://www.cdc.gov/healthyschools/obesity/index.htm

Centers for Disease Control and Prevention. (n.d.). *Sexual risk behaviors can lead to HIV, STDs, & teen pregnancy.* https://www.cdc.gov/healthyyouth/sexualbehaviors/index.htm

Centers for Disease Control and Prevention. (n.d.). *Sleep and sleep disorders: Data and statistics.* https://www.cdc.gov/sleep/data_statistics.html

Centers for Disease Control and Prevention. (2022, June 8). *Sleep and sleep disorders: Schools start too early.* https://www.cdc.gov/sleep/features/schools-start-too-early.html

Centers for Medicare & Medicaid Services. (n.d.). *The Mental Health Parity and Addiction Equity Act (MHPAEA).* https://www.cms.gov/CCIIO/Programs-and-Initiatives/Other-Insurance-Protections/mhpaea_factsheet

Chaput, J.-P., & Dutil, C. (2016). Lack of sleep as a contributor to obesity in adolescents: Impacts on eating and activity behaviors. *International Journal of Behavioral Nutrition and Physical Activity, 13.* https://doi.org/10.1186/s12966-016-0428-0

Clegg, N. (2021, September 18). *What the Wall Street Journal got wrong.* Meta. https://about.fb.com/news/2021/09/what-the-wall-street-journal-got-wrong/

Cohen, B. M., & Zubenko, G. S. (2019). Gene testing to guide antidepressant treatment: Has its time arrived? *Harvard Health Blog.* https://www.health.harvard.edu/blog/gene-testing-to-guide-antidepressant-treatment-has-its-time-arrived-2019100917964

Cole, E. J., Phillips, A. L., Bentzley, B. S., Stimpson, K. H., Nejad, R., Barmak, F., Veerapal, C., Khan, N., Cherian, K., Felber, E., Brown, R., Choi, E., King, S., Pankow, H., Bishop, J. H., Azeez, A., Coetzee, J., Rapier, R., Odenwald, N., . . . Williams, N. R. (2022). Stanford neuromodulation therapy (SNT): A double-blind randomized controlled trial. *The American Journal of Psychiatry, 179*(2), 132–141. https://doi.org/10.1176/appi.ajp.2021.20101429

Collyer, R., Clancy, A., & Borody, T. (2020, December). Faecal microbiota transplantation alleviates symptoms of depression in individuals with irritable bowel syndrome: A case series. *Medicine in Microecology, 6,* Article 100029. https://doi.org/10.1016/j.medmic.2020.100029

Cullen, K. R., Amatya, P., Roback, M. G., Albott, C. S., Westlund Schreiner, M., Ren, Y., Eberly, L. E., Carstedt, P., Samikoglu, A., Gunlicks-Stoessel, M., Reigstad, K., Horek, N., Tye, S., Lim, K. O., & Klimes-Dougan, B. (2018). Intravenous ketamine for adolescents with treatment-resistant depression: An open-label study. *Journal of Child and Adolescent Psychopharmacology, 28*(7), 437–444. https://doi.org/10.1089/cap.2018.0030.

Curtin, S. C. (2020). State suicide rates among adolescents and young adults aged 10–24: United States, 2000–2018. *National Vital Statistics Reports, 69*(11). https://www.cdc.gov/nchs/data/nvsr/nvsr69/nvsr-69-11-508.pdf

Curtin, S. C., & Heron, M. (2019, October). Death rates due to suicide and homicide among persons aged 10–24: United States, 2000–2017. *NCHS Data Brief, 352*. https://www.cdc.gov/nchs/data/databriefs/db352-h.pdf

Davenport, S., Gray, T. J., & Melek, S. P. (2019, November 20). *Addiction and mental health vs. physical health: Widening disparities in network use and provider reimbursement.* Milliman. https://www.milliman.com/en/insight/addiction-and-mental-health-vs-physical-health-widening-disparities-in-network-use-and-p

Davidson, R. J., & Lutz, A. (2008). Buddha's brain: Neuroplasticity and meditation. *IEEE Signal Processing Magazine, 25*(1), 174–176. https://doi.org/10.1109/msp.2008.4431873

Dembosky, A. (2021, November 18). *Americans can wait many weeks to see a therapist. California law aims to fix that.* NPR. https://www.npr.org/sections/health-shots/2021/11/18/1053566020/americans-can-wait-many-weeks-to-see-a-therapist-california-law-aims-to-fix-that

Dickson, C. (2015, February 5). *Bipolar teen's death in police station highlights rift between cops, mentally ill.* Yahoo! News. https://www.yahoo.com/entertainment/news/bipolar-teen-s-death-highlights-frequency-of-violent-encounters-between-police--mentally-ill-014049696.html?guccounter=1

Dickson, J. D. (2021, December 23). Prosecutor on Crumbley warning signs: Ethan had bird head in jar, mom had affair. *The Detroit News.* https://www.detroitnews.com/story/news/local/oakland-county/2021/12/23/prosecutor-ahead-bond-review-crumbleys-put-home-sale-sold-horses-and-pose-flight-risk/9010898002/

Doheny, K. (2011, January 10). *Optimism may protect teens against depression.* Grow by WebMD. https://www.webmd.com/parenting/news/20110110/optimism-may-protect-teens-against-depression

Dwyer, J. B., Landeros-Weisenberger, A., Johnson, J. A., Londono Tobon, A., Flores, J. M., Nasir, M., Couloures, K., Sanacora, G., & Bloch, M. H. (2021). Efficacy of intravenous ketamine in adolescent treatment-resistant depression: A randomized midazolam-controlled trial. *The American Journal of Psychiatry, 178*(4), 352–362. https://doi.org/10.1176/appi.ajp.2020.20010018

Eggleston, C., & Fields, J. (2021, March 22). *Census Bureau's Household Pulse Survey shows significant increase in homeschooling rates in Fall 2020.* United States Census Bureau. https://www.census.gov/library/stories/2021/03/homeschooling-on-the-rise-during-covid-19-pandemic.html

Ellison, K. (2020, March 28). E-therapy apps see booming business since coronavirus pandemic. I gave one a try. *The Washington Post.* https://www.washingtonpost.com/healthinclude/e-therapy-apps-see-booming-business-since-coronavirus-pandemic-i-gave-one-a-try/2020/03/27/985682c4-6d20-11ea-a3ec-70d7479d83f0_story.html

Ellison, K. (2021, March 27). Sleep-deprived kids have gotten a break with remote learning's later start times. Some hope it's a wake-up call for schools. *The Washington Post.* https://www.washingtonpost.com/health/teenage-sleep-remote-learning-school-time/2021/03/26/29d3c004-898b-11eb-8a8b-5cf82c3dffe4_story.html

Gaudiano, B. A., Dalrymple, K. L., & Zimmerman, M. (2009). Prevalence and clinical characteristics of psychotic versus nonpsychotic major depression in a general psychiatric outpatient clinic. *Depression and Anxiety, 26*(1), 54–64. https://doi.org/10.1002/da.20470.

Geiger, A. W., & Davis, L. (2019, July 12). *A growing number of American teenagers—particularly girls—are facing depression.* Pew Research Center. https://www.pewresearch.org/fact-tank/2019/07/12/a-growing-number-of-american-teenagers-particularly-girls-are-facing-depression/

Gentile, D. A., Reimer, R. A., Nathanson, A. I., Walsh, D. A., & Eisenmann, J. C. (2014, May). Protective effects of parental monitoring of children's media use: A prospective study. *JAMA Pediatrics, 168*(5), 479–484. https://doi.org/10.1001/jamapediatrics.2014.146

Goldstein, T. R., Krantz, M., Merranko, J., Garcia, M., Sobel, L., Rodriguez, C., Douaihy, A., Axelson, D., & Birmaher, B. (2016). Medication adherence among adolescents with bipolar disorder. *Journal of Child and Adolescent Psychopharmacology, 26*(10), 864–872. https://doi.org/10.1089/cap.2016.0030

Goodman, L. (n.d.). *Guidance for advocates: Identifying parity violations & taking action.* Health Law Advocates. https://www.communitycatalyst.org/resources/publications/document/parity-issue-brief-FINAL-12-9-14.pdf?1418154547

GoodTherapy. (2014). *How much does therapy cost?* https://www.goodtherapy.org/blog/faq/how-much-does-therapy-cost

Griswold, B. (2015, June 8). *Blue Shield of California and Magellan: A deceptive arrangement.* Navigating the Insurance Maze. https://theinsurancemaze.com/articles/magellan/

Hainey, M. (2018, November 27). Beneath the surface of Bruce Springsteen. *Esquire.* https://www.esquire.com/entertainment/a25133821/bruce-springsteen-interview-netflix-broadway-2018/

Hall-Flavin, D. K. (2018, November 17). *Antidepressants and weight gain: What causes it?* Mayo Clinic. https://www.mayoclinic.org/diseases-conditions/depression/expert-answers/antidepressants-and-weight-gain/faq-20058127

Harman, G., Kliamovich, D., Morales, A. M., Gilbert, S., Barch, D. M., Mooney, M. A., Ewing, S. W. F., Fair, D. A., & Nagel, B. J. (2021). Prediction of suicidal ideation and attempt in 9 and 10 year-old children using transdiagnostic risk features. *PLoS ONE, 16*(5), Article e0252114. https://doi.org/10.1371/journal.pone.0252114

Harvard Health Publishing. (2021, February 2). *Exercise is an all-natural treatment to fight depression.* https://www.health.harvard.edu/mind-and-mood/exercise-is-an-all-natural-treatment-to-fight-depression

Harvard Health Publishing. (2022, May 15). *Going off antidepressants.* https://www.health.harvard.edu/diseases-and-conditions/going-off-antidepressants

Heilmann, A., Mehay, A., Watt, R. G., Kelly, Y., Durrant, J. E., van Turnhout, J., & Gershoff, E. T. (2021). Physical punishment and child outcomes: A narrative review of prospective studies. *The Lancet, 398*(10297), 355–364. https://doi.org/10.1016/S0140-6736(21)00582-1

Hevesi, D. (2012, May 22). Katie Beckett, who inspired health reform, dies at 34. *The New York Times*. https://www.nytimes.com/2012/05/23/us/katie-beck ett-who-inspired-health-reform-dies-at-34.html

Holland, K., & Riley, E. (2017, October 11). *ADHD numbers: Facts, statistics, and you*. The ADD Resource Center. https://www.addrc.org/adhd-numbers-facts-sta tistics-and-you/

Hosseini, R. F. (2014, November 27). How Sacramento turns at-risk kids into criminals. *Sacramento News & Review*. https://www.newsreview.com/sacramento/ content/how-sacramento-turns-at-risk-kids-into-criminals/15590372/

Howell, B. A., Wang, E. A., & Winkelman, T. N. A. (2019). Mental health treatment among individuals involved in the criminal justice system after implementation of the Affordable Care Act. *Psychiatric Services*, *70*(9), 765–771. https:// doi.org/10.1176/appi.ps.201800559

Iervolino, S. (2021, July 8). *Simone Biles opens up about depression she suffered after being sexually abused*. GMA. https://www.goodmorningamerica.com/culture/ story/simone-biles-opens-depression-suffered-sexually-abused-78735393

Jacobson, R. (2022, July 28). *How to talk to your teen about substance use*. Child Mind Institute. https://childmind.org/article/talk-teenager-substance-use-abuse/

JED Foundation. (n.d.). *Supporting mental health from a distance: When should a parent intervene?* https://jedfoundation.org/set-to-go/supporting-mental-health-from-a-distance-when-should-a-parent-intervene/

Jick, H., Kaye, J. A., & Jick, S. S. (2004). Antidepressants and the risk of suicidal behaviors. *JAMA*, *292*(3), 338–343. https://doi.org/10.1001/jama.292.3.338

Joly, V. (2017, February 23). *Single case agreement (SCA) with insurance companies*. Vinodha Psychotherapy and Consultation. https://vinodhatherapy.com/blogs/ 2017/2/23/single-case-agreement-sca-with-insurance-companies

Kaplan, A. (2020, January 29). Does science support the "wilderness" in wilderness therapy? *Undark*. https://undark.org/2020/01/29/does-science-support-the-wil derness-in-wilderness-therapy/

Kaplan, K. (2018, November 8). A lot more Americans are meditating now than just five years ago. *Los Angeles Times*. https://www.latimes.com/science/sciencenow/ la-sci-sn-americans-meditating-more-20181108-story.html

Keane, D. (2021, 25 October). Molly Russell's father meets Facebook whistleblower Frances Haugen. *Evening Standard*. https://www.standard.co.uk/news/ uk/molly-russell-dad-teenager-suicide-facebook-whistblower-frances-haugen-b962289.html

Kwon, M., Seo, Y. S., Park, E., & Chang, Y-P. (2020). Association between substance use and insufficient sleep in U.S. high school students. *The Journal of School Nursing*, *37*(6). https://doi.org/10.1177/1059840519901161

Lambert, K. (2015). Do or diy. *RSA Journal*, *161*(5561), 20–23. https://www.jstor. org/stable/26204384

Lambert, K. (2018). Building the brain's contingency circuit. In *Well-grounded: The neurobiology of rational decisions* (pp. 73–94). Yale University Press.

LaMotte, S. (2020, July 29). *Spanking has declined in America, study finds, but pediatricians worry about impact of pandemic.* CNN. https://www.cnn.com/2020/07/27/health/spanking-decline-us-wellness/index.html

Lee, A. M. I. (n.d.). *What is a functional behavioral assessment (FBA)?* Understood. https://www.understood.org/en/articles/functional-assessment-what-it-is-and-how-it-works

Lee, C.-H., & Giuliani, F. (2019, July 19). The role of inflammation in depression and fatigue. *Frontiers in Immunology, 10,* Article 1696. https://doi.org/10.3389/fimmu.2019.01696

Lee, S., Rothbard, A. B., & Noll, E. L. (2012). Length of inpatient stay of persons with serious mental illness: Effects of hospital and regional characteristics. *Psychiatric Services, 63*(9), 889–895. https://doi.org/10.1176/appi.ps.201100412

Levine, M. (2008). *The price of privilege: How parental pressure and material advantage are creating a generation of disconnected and unhappy kids.* HarperCollins.

Limbana, T., Khan, F., & Eskander, N. (2020). Gut microbiome and depression: How microbes affect the way we think. *Cureus, 12*(8), Article e9966. https://doi.org/10.7759/cureus.9966

MacPhee, J., Modi, K., Gorman, S., Roy, N., Riba, E., Cusumano, D., Dunkle, J., Komrosky, N., Schwartz, V., Eisenberg, D., Silverman, M. M., Pinder-Amaker, S., Watkins, K. B., & Doraiswamy, P. M. (2021, June 21). *A comprehensive approach to mental health promotion and suicide prevention for colleges and universities: Insights from the JED campus program.* National Academy of Medicine. https://nam.edu/wp-content/uploads/2021/06/A-Comprehensive-Approach-to-Mental-Health-Promotion-and-Suicide-Prevention.pdf

Makin, S. (2019, April 12). Behind the buzz: How ketamine changes the depressed patient's brain. *Scientific American.* https://www.scientificamerican.com/article/behind-the-buzz-how-ketamine-changes-the-depressed-patients-brain/

Marcus, D. L. (2006). *What it takes to pull me through: Why teenagers get in trouble—and how four of them got out.* Harper Paperbacks.

Martini, R., Hilt, R., Marx, L., Chenven, M., Naylor, M., Sarvet, B., & Ptakowski, K. K. (2012, June). *Best principles for integration of child psychiatry into the pediatric health home.* American Academy of Child & Adolescent Psychiatry. https://www.aacap.org/App_Themes/AACAP/docs/clinical_practice_center/systems_of_care/best_principles_for_integration_of_child_psychiatry_into_the_pediatric_health_home_2012.pdf

Marylanders to Prevent Gun Violence. (n.d.). *Maryland safe storage map.* https://mdpgv.org/safestoragemap/

Mayo Clinic. (2020, November 18). *SAMe.* https://www.mayoclinic.org/drugs-supplements-same/art-20364924

McCallion, G., & Feder, J. (2013, October 18). *Student bullying: Overview of research, federal initiatives, and legal issues.* Congressional Research Service report. https://sgp.fas.org/crs/misc/R43254.pdf

Mehren, E. (1990, August 28). Memoir of madness: William Styron details the "horror of depression" in his new book. *Los Angeles Times*. https://www.latimes.com/archives/la-xpm-1990-08-28-vw-189-story.html

Mental Daily. (2021, July 3). *Physical activity found to be more beneficial than previously known for brain health of children*. https://www.mentaldaily.com/article/2021/07/physical-activity-found-to-be-more-beneficial-than-previously-known-for-brain-health-of-children

Mental Health America. (2018). *The state of mental health in America 2018*. https://www.mhanational.org/issues/state-mental-health-america-2018

MichiganMom. (2016, October 21). *How I survived parenting a teen with depression*. HuffPost. https://www.huffpost.com/entry/how-i-survived-parenting-a-teen-with-depression_b_5809d8b1e4b099c43431940f

Miller, L., Wickramaratne, P., Hao, X., McClintock, C. H., Pan, L., Svob, C., & Weissman, M. M. (2021). Altruism and "love of neighbor" offer neuroanatomical protection against depression. *Psychiatry Research: Neuroimaging, 315*, Article 111326. https://doi.org/10.1016/j.pscychresns.2021.111326

Morin, A. (n.d.). *9 steps to take if your request for evaluation is denied*. Understood. https://www.understood.org/en/articles/9-steps-to-take-if-your-request-for-evaluation-is-denied

Muzaffar, N., Brito, E. B., Fogel, J., Fagan, D., Kumar, K., & Verma, R. (2018). The association of adolescent Facebook behaviours with symptoms of social anxiety, generalized anxiety, and depression. *Journal of the Canadian Academy of Child and Adolescent Psychiatry, 27*(4), 252–260.

National Alliance on Mental Illness. (2022, June). *Mental health by the numbers*. https://www.nami.org/mhstats

National Institutes of Health. (2021, June 22). *Cannabis use may be associated with suicidality in young adults*. US Department of Health and Human Services. https://www.nih.gov/news-events/news-releases/cannabis-use-may-be-associated-suicidality-young-adults

National Institute of Mental Health. (2022, January). *Major depression*. US Department of Health and Human Services. https://www.nimh.nih.gov/health/statistics/major-depression

Office of Juvenile Justice and Delinquency Prevention. (2017, July). *Intersection between mental health and the juvenile justice system*. https://ojjdp.ojp.gov/model-programs-guide/literature-reviews/intsection_between_mental_health_and_the_juvenile_justice_system.pdf

Office of the US Surgeon General. (2021, December 7). *Protecting youth mental health: The U.S. Surgeon General's advisory*. https://www.hhs.gov/sites/default/files/surgeon-general-youth-mental-health-advisory.pdf

Pandey, E. (2021, August 31). *Homeschooling reaches critical mass*. Axios. https://www.axios.com/2021/08/31/homeschooling-pandemic-critical-mass

Parikh, T., & Walkup, J. T. (2021). The future of ketamine in the treatment of teen depression. *The American Journal of Psychiatry, 178*(4), 288–289. https://ajp.psychiatryonline.org/doi/pdf/10.1176/appi.ajp.2020.21020172

Parks, C. (2021, June 14). The rise of Black homeschooling. *The New Yorker.* https://www.newyorker.com/magazine/2021/06/21/the-rise-of-black-homeschooling

Pearson, D. G., & Craig, T. (2014, October 21). The great outdoors? Exploring the mental health benefits of natural environments. *Frontiers in Psychology.* https://doi.org/10.3389/fpsyg.2014.01178

Peru, G. (2022, January 20). *The best sunlight lamps for winter depression and light therapy.* MUO. https://www.makeuseof.com/tag/light-therapy-beat-winter-depression/

Pizza, F., Contardi, S., Antognini, A. B., Zagoraiou, M., Borrotti, M., Mostacci, B., Mondini, S., & Cirignotta, F. (2010). Sleep quality and motor vehicle crashes in adolescents. *Journal of Clinical Sleep Medicine, 6*(1), 41–45.

ProCon.org. (2022, June 6). *State-by-state recreational marijuana laws.* https://marijuana.procon.org/legal-recreational-marijuana-states-and-dc

Ray, B. D. (2022, March 26). *Homeschooling: The research.* National Home Education Research Institute. https://www.nheri.org/research-facts-on-homeschooling/

Rivers, I., Poteat, V. P., Noret, N., & Ashurst, N. (2009). Observing bullying at school: The mental health implications of witness status. *School Psychology Quarterly, 24*(4), 211–223. https://doi.org/10.1037/a0018164

Rudgard, O. (2018, November 6). The tech moguls who invented social media have banned their children from it. *Independent.* https://www.independent.ie/life/family/parenting/the-tech-moguls-who-invented-social-media-have-banned-their-children-from-it-37494367.html

Ryan, C. (2009). *Helping families support their lesbian, gay, bisexual, and transgender (LGBT) children.* Georgetown University. https://nccc.georgetown.edu/documents/LGBT_Brief.pdf

Ryan, C., Huebner, D., Diaz, R. M., & Sanchez, J. (2009). Family rejection as a predictor of negative health outcomes in white and Latino lesbian, gay, and bisexual young adults. *Pediatrics, 123*(1), 346–352. https://doi.org/10.1542/peds.2007-3524

Savioja, H., Helminen, M., Fröjd, S., Marttunen, M., & Kaltiala-Heino, R. (2015). Sexual experience and self-reported depression across the adolescent years. *Health Psychology and Behavioral Medicine, 3*(1), 337–347. https://doi.org/10.1080/21642850.2015.1101696

Second Nature. (2019, October 10). *Is it time for wilderness therapy?* https://www.second-nature.com/blog/is-it-time-for-wilderness-therapy

Sheff, D. (2017, May). *I thought addiction was my son's problem. But addiction is a family disease.* Partnership to End Addiction. https://drugfree.org/parent-blog/i-thought-addiction-was-my-sons-problem-but-addiction-is-a-family-disease/

Shem, S. (1978). *The house of God.* Penguin.

Shim, R. S. (2021, July). Dismantling structural racism in psychiatry: A path to mental health equity. *The American Journal of Psychiatry, 178*(7), 592–598. https://doi.org/10.1176/appi.ajp.2021.21060558

Sobowale, K., & Ross, D. A. (2018). Poverty, parenting, and psychiatry. *Biological Psychiatry, 84*(5), e29–e31. https://doi.org/10.1016/j.biopsych.2018.07.007

Stallard, P., Spears, M., Montgomery, A. A., Phillips, R., & Sayal, K. (2013). Self-harm in young adolescents (12–16 years): Onset and short-term continuation in a community sample. *BMC Psychiatry, 13*, Article 328. https://doi.org/10.1186/1471-244X-13-328.

Substance Abuse and Mental Health Services Administration. (n.d.). *Know the risks of marijuana.* https://www.samhsa.gov/marijuana

Thomas, K. C., Shartzer, A., Kurth, N. K., & Hall, J. P. (2018, February 1). Impact of ACA health reforms for people with mental health conditions. *Psychiatric Services, 69*(2), 231–234. https://doi.org/10.1176/appi.ps.201700044

Turgay, A., & Ansari, R. (2006, April). Major depression with ADHD in children and adolescents. *Psychiatry, 3*(4), 20–32.

Typaldos, M., & Glaze, D. G. (n.d.). *Teenagers: Sleep patterns and school performance.* National Healthy Sleep Awareness Project. https://sleepeducation.org/wp-content/uploads/2021/04/teenssleeppatternsandschoolperformance.pdf

US Food and Drug Administration. (2018, February 5). *Suicidality in children and adolescents being treated with antidepressant medications.* https://www.fda.gov/drugs/postmarket-drug-safety-information-patients-and-providers/suicidality-children-and-adolescents-being-treated-antidepressant-medications

Utter, J., Denny, S., Peiris-John, R., Moselen, E., Dyson, B., & Clark, T. (2017, January 1). Family meals and adolescent emotional well-being: Findings from a national study. *Journal of Nutrition Education and Behavior, 49*(1), 67–72. https://doi.org/10.1016/j.jneb.2016.09.002

Variety. (2019, July 16). *"13 Reasons Why" edits controversial suicide scene.* NBC News. https://www.nbcnews.com/pop-culture/tv/13-reasons-why-edits-controversial-suicide-scene-n1030241

Waldorf School of St. Louis. (n.d.) *Waldorf School of St. Louis media and technology philosophy.* https://www.waldorfstl.org/media-and-technology

Walker, R. (2019). *Advice I ignored: Stories and wisdom from a formerly depressed teen* Ruby Walker.

Watson, J. (n.d.). *Wilderness therapy programs: A comprehensive guide for parents.* Aspiro Adventure Therapy. https://aspiroadventure.com/wilderness-therapy-programs/

Whitmire, R. (2019, April 8). *Alarming statistics tell the story behind America's college completion crisis: Nearly a third of all college students still don't have a degree six years later.* The 74. https://www.the74million.org/article/alarming-statistics-tell-the-story-behind-americas-college-completion-crisis-nearly-a-third-of-all-college-student-still-dont-have-a-degree-six-years-later/

Wright, K. P., Linton, S. K., Withrow, D., Casiraghi, L., Lanza, S. M., de la Iglesia, H., Vetter, C., & Depne, C. M. (2020). Sleep in university students prior to and during COVID-19 stay-at-home orders. *Current Biology, 30*. https://www.cell.com/current-biology/pdf/S0960-9822(20)30838-1.pdf

Zakrzewski, C., & Lima, C. (2021, October 4). Former Facebook employee Frances Haugen revealed as "whistleblower" behind leaked documents that plunged the company into scandal. *The Washington Post.* https://www.washingtonpost.com/technology/2021/10/03/facebook-whistleblower-frances-haugen-revealed/

Index